# The Economics of a Breakaway Football League

Throughout the history of football, new leagues have periodically emerged offering high salaries to lure foreign stars—the United States, Japan, and China being prominent examples. Less well known, however, is the case of Colombia. The Colombian professional football league was a brief but remarkable experiment that attracted top South American and European players in the early 1950s, commonly referred to as El Dorado.

Drawing on a wide array of archival material and other primary sources, this book explores how a small, economically underdeveloped country with no established football tradition managed to finance such a high-profile "pirate" league while confronting the international football establishment. It examines the economic and social conditions that made it possible to field world-class players such as Alfredo Di Stéfano and Charlie Mitten, and explicitly addresses the domestic and international circumstances that allowed so powerful a league to emerge so far from football's traditional centers of power.

This book also traces the collapse of the league and its lasting ramifications for the history of football in the region. It will be of great interest to readers in sports economics, sports history, economic history, and Latin American studies.

**Jorge Tovar** is a Full Professor in the Department of Economics at Universidad de Los Andes, Bogota, Colombia.

**Andrés Álvarez** an Associate Professor in the Department of Economics at Universidad de Los Andes, Bogota, Colombia.

## Routledge Focus on Economics and Finance

The fields of economics are constantly expanding and evolving. This growth presents challenges for readers trying to keep up with the latest important insights. Routledge Focus on Economics and Finance presents short books on the latest big topics, linking in with the most cutting-edge economics research.

Individually, each title in the series provides coverage of a key academic topic, whilst collectively the series forms a comprehensive collection across the whole spectrum of economics.

**Proactivity in Economics**
Between Resourcefulness and Entrepreneurship
*Jakub Bożydar Wiśniewski*

**The Geoeconomics of Global Value Chains**
Navigating Geopolitical Complexity and Industrial Policy Shifts
*Katarzyna Mroczek-Dąbrowska*

**Dollar Dominance**
Fundamentals, Nature and Present Structure
*Junji Tokunaga*

**Resilient Global Supply Chains and Geopolitical Risk**
Evidence from Central and Eastern Europe
*Aleksandra Kania*

**Interest Rates and Asset Values**
A Case Study in Closed Markets
*Richard Thomas*

**Green Fiscal Policy and Firm Behaviour**
Towards Energy Efficiency
*Kinga B. Tchórzewska*

For more information about this series, please visit: www.routledge.com/Routledge-Focus-on-Economics-and-Finance/book-series/RFEF

# The Economics of a Breakaway Football League

## The Rise and Fall of Colombia's El Dorado in the 1950s

**Jorge Tovar and Andrés Álvarez**

Routledge
Taylor & Francis Group
LONDON AND NEW YORK

First published 2027
by Routledge
4 Park Square, Milton Park, Abingdon, Oxon OX14 4RN

and by Routledge
605 Third Avenue, New York, NY 10158

*Routledge is an imprint of the Taylor & Francis Group, an informa business*



*British Library Cataloguing-in-Publication Data*
A catalogue record for this book is available from the British Library

ISBN: 978-1-032-49906-2 (hbk)
ISBN: 978-1-032-49912-3 (pbk)
ISBN: 978-1-003-39602-4 (ebk)

DOI: 10.4324/9781003396024

Typeset in Times New Roman
by codeMantra

**Jorge dedicates this book to Laura.**

***May the legends and enchantment of football's vanished world speak to my cherished reader who hungers for adventure and fiction.***

**Andrés dedicates this book to the memory of Benito**

***For his goals, and the Guaraní grit that made our family fall in love with football.***

# Contents

# Figures

# Acknowledgments

We are grateful to many people and institutions that have helped us complete this book. We thank the North American Society for Sport History (NASSH) for granting us the 2023 American Sport History Grant, which allowed us to visit Argentina. In Argentina, we thank Esteban Beckerman and Nicolás Mirelman, the latter for his helpful cooperation during our visit to the River Plate Archive. In Lima, we appreciate José Gallardo's help, Professor at the Pontificia Universidad Católica del Perú, while visiting Lima and easing access to the University's Instituto Riva Agüero. In Barranquilla, Erika Fontalvo, Director of Barranquilla's El Heraldo, kindly granted us access to the newspaper's historical archive.

Stefan Szymanski, Professor of Sport Management at the University of Michigan, Ann Arbor, and Victor Hugo Kurhy, from Argentina, shared valuable information about English and Argentine clubs and leagues, respectively. We also value Hernán Peláez's willingness to speak with us about his experience with El Dorado.

We want to thank the discussants and participants at the 2023 1st Latin American Sports Economics Conference (Universidad de Los Andes, Bogota, Colombia), the 2024 3rd Reading Football Economics Conference (University of Reading, United Kingdom), the 2024 10th Football & Finance Conference (University of Duisburg, Germany), and the 2025 16th European Sports Economics Conference (Innsbruck, Austria).

We recognize María Paula Vargas, Alejandra Isabel Zakzuk, and Juan Camilo Díaz for their research assistance at early stages. We thank Francisco Espinel for his assistance in collecting documents from the Banco de la República's press archives in Manizales.

Jorge wishes to acknowledge Hermes, Gilma, Andrea, Laura, and Tatiana for their continuous support and encouragement over the years it took to write this book.

Andrés wishes to acknowledge the enthusiastic encouragement and the supportive expectations of Jimena, Mauricio, and Eduardo.

# 1 How come Colombia?

## When myth meets reality

Myths constitute legends, and fantastical narratives about events that societies create and reproduce as realities belonging to their foundational times. These magic worlds have emerged in every culture and society. When Europeans arrived in the Americas in the sixteenth century, they carried in their minds multiple legends that led them to search for the spiritual kingdom of Gran Paititi and to track down a city of gold in the Amazon. After the conquest of Peru, given the immense quantity of precious metals that constituted Atahualpa's ransom in 1532, the conquistadors advanced from the Caribbean coast toward the interior of present-day Colombia, where they encountered the legend of El Dorado. With gold abundant, it was the Chibcha people in the Andes who told the Spaniards about the cacique of Guatavita bathing in a lagoon covered in gold. The search for El Dorado kept on shifting, from Guiana, which Hernán Pérez de Quesada attempted to find in the 1540s, to a golden region which Gonzalo Jiménez de Quesada sought in the 1570s. Despite the continuous and subsequent expeditions, El Dorado vanished into the ambitions and dreams of the conquistadors.

Yet the dream of Guatavita Lake persisted. With millions in gold said to lie motionless at the bottom of the lagoon, just 65 kilometers north of present-day Bogota—no surprise what happened next. The Spaniards set out to empty it, drain it, and obtain the unimaginable wealth. But they failed. Later, after independence, the English created companies to drain the lagoon and collect the treasure of El Dorado. Even in the twentieth century, English companies employing new technologies attempted to dry the lagoon but found it impossible. By the mid-twentieth century, nothing remained of those fantastic dreams but the legend itself—El Dorado as pure myth. In reality, the myth had long since been reduced to the pursuit and plunder of whatever gold the conquistadors found among the native peoples in their path. El Dorado, it turned out, was everywhere and nowhere: scattered across the continent rather than concentrated in one magical place.

DOI: 10.4324/9781003396024-1

If El Dorado began as a legend based on partial truths, the name reappeared in mid-twentieth-century Colombia as a football myth, closely associated with one club above all others: Bogota's Los Millonarios. In the colonial story, gold existed but was scattered; the search for one mountain or city of vast wealth turned those scattered resources into a story of conquest and discovery. The football El Dorado followed a similar pattern. It offered unusually high rewards to a new group of outsiders—players arriving from South America and Europe—and their presence in Colombia strengthened the idea that the country briefly hosted one of the world's strongest leagues. Yet, as in the earlier legend, the episode is often reduced to a single, overly simple explanation.

The tale of El Dorado follows a common narrative: the league brought in top-level players following a strike in Argentina.[1] To fully understand El Dorado, one needs to consider the football labor markets in South America and even England. It is also necessary to grasp how geography and internal cultural differences have shaped the nation, and how football reflects Colombia's society. El Dorado is arguably one of the first events of qualified workers' migration registered in the twentieth century.

El Dorado is the story of a rogue league that challenged FIFA's growing status. Lacking governmental official support, the league represented, between 1949 and 1953, the history of a humble boy who became a knight. Football is at its center, with Millonarios being the most representative club. Other teams, including Cali, Santa Fe, Boca Juniors, and Quindío, also managed to expand the legend of El Dorado beyond its borders.

To date, there has been no systematic analysis of the financial sustainability of the Colombian league. The clubs invested in trying to mirror Millonarios' successful strategy—bringing in the best and playing in packed stadiums—but talent is scarce, and even with great names, most clubs were unable to replicate it.

The difficulties were not only domestic, but the South American Football Confederation (CONMEBOL) and FIFA also pushed hard to bring Colombia back into line. Argentina never pardoned its players for leaving illegally for Colombia. Peru, the other heavy supplier of players, had a different approach. They introduced professional football and pardoned its players, thereby incentivizing their return.

The league came into being because domestic football was insufficient to raise the funds needed to maintain the expensive roster. Although the teams were able to play some friendly games, the Colombian league was not enough to raise the money required to pay its stars. South American countries, led by Peru and Argentina and under FIFA scrutiny, pushed hard for an agreement. In October 1951, the Lima Pact allowed Colombian clubs to retain their players until October 1954. It was then that the legend of El Dorado became universal. For around two years, the Colombian clubs played against many of the most powerful teams in South America and against a team that would come to be the best club of the twentieth century: Real Madrid.

The boom nevertheless contained the conditions of its own contraction. Despite the mythology of permanent sell-outs and limitless revenues, the league's finances depended on a narrow set of income streams that were not deep enough across most cities to sustain the payrolls.

The pact marked the beginning of the end. With many of its stars having arrived between mid-1949 and October 1951, the peak was 1952. The borders were not completely closed, but in practice, no major star arrived after the Lima Pact. And many left, legally, illegally, or in some middle-ground discussion. When Di Stéfano, the best of all, left during the 1953 preseason, one could say that El Dorado was over.

We propose a two-fold interpretation: economic and historical. El Dorado resembled a speculative cycle in a young entertainment industry: an initial "first-mover" advantage, widespread imitation by clubs that lacked the relevant scale, and a market correction once the regulatory environment and revenue constraints became binding. We reconstructed it using extensive archival work and a new dataset that captures not only official matches but also the dense universe of friendlies and tours that sustained the league's business model.

Using primary sources and numerous digital sources, we built a unique dataset comprising almost every game, both friendly and official, played by Colombian teams between 1948 and 1953. For all these matches, we have information on the final score and venue, and for many, we also collected data on attendance and gate receipts. Moreover, we have scattered information about the financial status of the Colombian clubs during the period of interest. Drawing on this rich body of evidence, we offer what may be the most detailed account of El Dorado, arguably of any mid-twentieth-century football league.

The main finding is that behind the golden goals scored by the stars of El Dorado, the league was never financially sustainable. Moreover, despite the legendary stories of full stadiums with glorious players dancing on the field for the delight of some impressed spectators, the truth was that this was true only systematically for Millonarios. Some of the other teams had periods of success and glory, but all faced financial difficulties. A significant conclusion is that money can buy happiness, and it did for a short period of time, but in the long run, without the necessary economic structure to sustain an industry, it was not viable to keep the operations going.

Tracking the dollar value of player transfers requires monitoring the evolution of exchange rates in Argentina and Colombia. The latter is straightforward owing to its stability. In the former, however, there was an exchange-rate adjustment in October 1949, when the "peso maintained its previous relationship with respect to the pound but was devalued in relation to the dollar, to stimulate exports in free foreign currency".[2] It was an 88% devaluation, which we incorporated into our estimates effective October 1, 1949. To present prices and players' values, we used the nominal domestic currency and converted to nominal dollars at the exchange rate (Table 5.1). This strategy allows us to compare values across the book and to assess price differentials across countries.

We offer a new account of El Dorado grounded in archival evidence and in a dataset that is both original and, to our knowledge, the first to assemble the episode's quantitative record in a systematic, exhaustive, and methodologically transparent way. We built this dataset from match records, attendance records, gate receipts, and scattered financial information, cross-checking across sources whenever possible.

## The historical background of El Dorado: Colombia in transition

In 1950, an international mission appointed by the World Bank, led by Lauchlin Currie, described Colombia as being in a period of transition from a static, feudal, and isolated economy to a more dynamic, national, and interdependent one, amid "social and political changes".[3] The report stressed that recent economic advances were real yet uneven, and that modern sectors in banking, industry, and infrastructure coexisted with a large poor population.

This picture of a society in transition is a useful starting point for understanding the environment in which Colombian professional football was born. During the late 1940s and early 1950s, Colombia experienced structural economic change, rapid demographic growth, accelerated urbanization, political radicalization, and a reconfiguration of its territorial economy.

El Dorado blossomed during a period of new capital flows generated by import-substitution industrialization, monetary stability underpinned by coffee exports, and an air transport network that connected a polycentric urban system. At the same time, most of the population remained poor, inequality was high, and the consolidation of a working urban middle class—with enough purchasing power to sustain football through gate receipts—was still incomplete. The urbanization process underway in Colombia was far from the industrial societies that supported the earlier rise of professional football in Britain, the Río de la Plata, and coastal Brazil.

The first half of the twentieth century was a pivotal period for Colombia's economy and politics. It was a coffee-driven foreign-exchange–dependent economy with a new regional entrepreneurial elite willing to invest surplus capital in sports. This coincided with the availability of top players driven out of neighboring leagues by economic and institutional crises. Although these conditions were sufficient to generate an extraordinary football experiment, they did not constitute a strong social and economic base capable of sustaining such a league in the long term.

To situate El Dorado within this broader economic and social process, we examine the political tensions that culminated in *La Violencia*, analyze the ongoing macroeconomic conditions, and review the social transformations associated with demographic change and urbanization. To fully understand any economic or social event in Colombia, one needs to understand the country's geography and the historical inability of its inhabitants to deal with its complexities.

### *Political instability*

Since the nineteenth century, partisan conflict between Liberals and Conservatives had periodically escalated into civil war. The "Regeneration" of the late nineteenth century created a centralist, Catholic, and conservative political order, but it did not resolve underlying tensions over land, regional autonomy, and the Church's role in public life.

The Liberal Republic (1930–1946) marked a partial break. Governments led by Olaya Herrera (1930–1934), López Pumarejo (1934–1938; 1942–1945), and Santos (1938–1942) sought to modernize institutions, expand citizenship, and implement a moderate reformist agenda. López implemented during his first presidential period agrarian and labor reforms while encouraging unions and peasant organizations. These measures, which generated fierce opposition from landowners, conservative elites, and segments of the Church, were only partially implemented in a country marked by highly concentrated land ownership and weak state capacity.[4]

By the mid-1940s, partisan polarization had intensified. The Conservative Party's return to the presidency in 1946, under Ospina Pérez, occurred amid growing social mobilization and deepening rural conflicts. Liberal dissidence crystallized around Jorge Eliécer Gaitán, whose discourse combined denunciations of oligarchic privilege with appeals to the urban poor and rural tenants. Gaitán's rise suggested the possibility of a populist realignment similar to those in Argentina, Brazil, or Mexico, but in Colombia, that path was brutally interrupted.

On April 9, 1948, Gaitán was assassinated in Bogota. The event triggered the *Bogotazo*, a massive riot that devastated the city and revealed the fragility of state authority. What had been, up to that point, a conflict rooted mainly in rural areas entered the capital with unprecedented force. The following years saw an escalation of partisan violence—*La Violencia*—in which rural communities, small towns, and some urban neighborhoods became battlegrounds for armed groups loosely associated with Liberal and Conservative factions. Estimates of the death toll exceeded 200,000 people during the following decade.

The political system oscillated between attempts at institutional negotiation and episodes of authoritarian control, culminating in the military coup of Rojas Pinilla in 1953. Even as parts of the economy expanded, the state struggled to control the violence or to provide basic security in vast rural areas. The conflict resulted in an active driver of social change, accelerating rural–urban migration, and deepening mistrust between social groups.

Professional football was born amid this atmosphere of polarization and uncertainty. The stadium, the Sunday match, and the radio broadcast offered forms of collective gathering that, at least temporarily, allowed identities to be articulated along lines other than party color. At the same time, the violence that pushed peasants toward the cities also limited public authorities' capacity to provide housing, transport, and services for the newcomers, constraining the emergence of a broad, solvent spectator base.

### *Economic conditions and development*

If the political climate of mid-century Colombia was unstable, its macroeconomic regime looked, from the outside, relatively orthodox and predictable. Historical reconstructions of GDP per capita place Colombia near the middle of the Latin American distribution by 1950, below Argentina and Chile, but above Brazil and close to Mexico.[5] Over the first half of the twentieth century, real GDP grew at an average of around 4%–4.5% per year, translating into per-capita gains of just over 2% annually.[6] Colombia was an intermediate performer converging slowly toward the regional mean.

Since the early twentieth century, coffee had become the dominant export crop, integrating Colombia into world markets and financing the expansion of banking, transport, and manufacturing. The post-war coffee boom, marked by rising international coffee prices and expanding volumes, produced a substantial inflow of foreign exchange. These dollars financed imports of machinery and intermediate goods, allowing the authorities to accumulate reserves and cushion the balance of payments.

As the coffee industry grew, other areas of the economy blossomed, changing the country's production structure. The share of manufacturing in GDP almost doubled between 1929 and 1945, rising from roughly 9% to around 16%–17%.[7] Antioquia, Bogotá, and Valle del Cauca emerged as industrial and commercial hubs, increasing their economic weight relative to more rural departments.

Unlike in several Southern Cone economies, where aggressive state-led industrialization was often financed through chronic inflation, exchange-rate overvaluation, and large fiscal deficits, Colombian industrialization in these years was more gradual and more tightly constrained by orthodox monetary policy. Between the mid-1940s and early 1950s, the peso fluctuated in a relatively narrow band against the US dollar. In contrast, the Argentine peso and the Brazilian cruzeiro lost much of their value under the pressure of high inflation and recurrent devaluations. This stability seemed to mark Colombia out within a region characterized by monetary turbulence. Currie's team emphasized the risks of financing investment through inflation, but they nonetheless noted that the country had avoided the worst macroeconomic imbalances of its neighbors.[8]

This macroeconomic configuration is central to understanding the financial foundations of El Dorado. For a professional footballer from Buenos Aires or Montevideo in the late 1940s, the prospect of being paid in Colombia, backed by coffee-generated dollars and managed by a relatively conservative central bank, was attractive compared to the uncertainties of an inflation-prone domestic currency. At the same time, coffee revenues and industrial profits were enriching a new business class in Bogota, Medellin, and Cali. These regional elites had both the liquidity and the ambition to invest in visible, prestige-generating projects. Professional football clubs—high-risk, high-profile ventures that could convert economic capital into symbolic capital—were one of the channels through which these surpluses were deployed.

### *Social change, urbanization, and the new urban classes*

Economic growth and monetary stability did not translate automatically into broad prosperity. Demographically, Colombia entered the mid-century in the midst of an accelerated transition. Research on the country's demographic history shows that, from the 1930s onward, mortality—especially infant and child mortality—declined sharply due to improvements in public health, vaccination, and basic sanitation, while fertility remained high for several decades.[9] Colombia's population rose from roughly 4 million at the turn of the century to more than 11 million by 1950, and projected continued rapid growth.[10]

These demographic shifts expanded the potential labor force, yet the modern economy struggled to absorb the new workers. Although employment in industry, construction, and public administration grew significantly, by mid-century the number of people in "informal" or low-productivity occupations already exceeded the combined workforce of those formal sectors.[11] The balance between capital accumulation and population growth generated urban underemployment and a structurally segmented labor market.

Urbanization accelerated under the combined pressure of demographic growth, rural poverty, and political violence. In 1905, only Bogota surpassed 80,000 inhabitants, representing about 2.5% of the national population. At the time, Medellin, Cali, and Barranquilla together accounted for barely 2% more. By the 1938 census, nearly 31% of Colombians lived in municipal capitals; over the following decades, this share continued to rise, and the largest growth occurred in the main urban centers.[12] The critical inflection occurred in the late 1940s and 1950s, when *La Violencia* displaced peasants from the land and into cities that were unprepared to meet the housing, water, sewage, and transportation needs they faced.

The Currie Mission emphasized that a large proportion of urban dwellers occupied overcrowded, precarious housing with limited access to piped water or sanitation, and that many Colombians' diets were poor in both quantity and quality. The country's social services and urban infrastructure lagged dangerously behind demographic realities, and poverty was a multidimensional problem involving low productivity, inadequate education, deficient health, and a precarious housing stock.[13]

Economic growth in mid-century Colombia thus occurred amid worsening inequality and a declining relative wage share. Historical accounts suggest that, after a recovery from the Great Depression, urban real wages grew only moderately from the 1930s to the early 1950s, with a more substantial surge only after 1957.[14]

For most urban workers during El Dorado, disposable income remained low and consumption opportunities constrained, in a world where price fluctuations were not negligible. Thus, in 1949, inflation increased by 33.3% for low-income households and 9.8% for middle-income households relative to 1948. The figure for the former decreased from 25% in 1950 to 0% in 1951, while middle-income households faced inflation rates of 17.8% in 1950 and 3.8% in 1951. In 1952, prices increased 15% for low-income households and 13.04% in 1953. In contrast, middle-income households faced an inflation rate of 1.8% in 1952 and 7.1% in 1953.[15] Prices increased faster for low-income families, which, if we follow modern patterns and given the informality already embedded in the labor market, probably earned below the COP 60 (USD 30) minimum wage set between 1950 and 1953.

Football ticket prices varied during El Dorado. In 1949, for instance, a ticket price in Barranquilla cost COP 2 (USD 1.02) to see a game between Deportivo Barranquilla and Universidad in the shadow stands. Women, children, and those willing to face the sun had to pay COP 1 (USD 0.51).[16] The prices in Barranquilla increased, reaching in 1951 COP 5 (USD 2) for a shadow stand and COP 2 (USD 0.8) for sun. Children under 3 would pay COP 3 (USD 1.2), and the rest of the Children would pay COP 1 (USD 0.4).[17] One wonders, of course, what explains charging more for under 10, but the overall picture is that prices increased while the minimum salary remained fixed.

In Bogota, meanwhile, in 1949, tickets for the Millonarios versus Santa Fe match cost COP 4 (USD 2) for "preferential", COP 3 (USD 1.5) on the West stands, COP 2 (USD 1) on the East, and COP 1 (USD 0.5) for North and South.[18] The prices changed, but not radically, when Millonarios played in the smaller "Alfonso López" stadium: COP 5 (USD 2.0), COP 4 (USD 1.6), and COP 3 (USD 1.2) in a game against Quindío.[19] The prices for the Real Madrid visit in 1952 were slightly higher, ranging from a high-priced ticket at COP 6 (USD 2.41) to a cheap one at COP 1.5 (USD 0.6), with tickets at COP 3 (USD 1.2), COP 4,5 (USD 1.8), and COP 5 (USD 2) in between.

It follows that football was accessible to the popular class, considering that for a minimum-wage earner, one day's work was worth COP 2 (USD 1) at the time. Still, it was not cheap, but as a new working class emerged in the cities, the base for football support increased. From the perspective of football history, this social structure is crucial. Classic studies of the sport in Britain and the Río de la Plata have emphasized that professional leagues and mass spectatorship depend on two overlapping social conditions: a sizable urban working class with some discretionary income and leisure time, and an emergent urban middle class willing to consume modern spectacles and media.[20] In Buenos Aires, Montevideo, or São Paulo, these conditions were in place by the 1920s and 1930s, supported by higher levels of urbanization and industrial employment. In Colombia, they were still taking shape in the late 1940s.

By 1950, cities like Bogota, Medellin, and Cali had grown rapidly, forming industrial belts and new working-class neighborhoods. Yet much of the urban labor force was employed in low-productivity services or informal activities, with limited capacity to attend matches regularly or to sustain high ticket prices. The urban middle class was expanding but remained numerically modest and socially fragmented. Inequality meant that a considerable share of the income gains generated by growth accrued to a relatively small elite.

Professional football thus emerged in a society where the idea of a mass urban public already existed—nourished by radio, newspapers, and the imagery of international football—but where the material base of that public was still fragile. The wages paid to foreign stars during El Dorado depended less on a broad base of paying spectators than on the investment decisions of a new industrial and commercial elite, often motivated by regional rivalry and prestige. When external conditions changed and those elites faced tighter constraints, the league's economic foundations eroded. In this sense, the brevity of El Dorado is not simply a matter of FIFA sanctions or coffee-price cycles. It also reflects the incomplete nature of Colombia's urban and class transition at mid-century.

### *A polycentric and rough geography and regionalism*

The territorial configuration of Colombia added another layer of specificity to this historical context. While Argentina, Uruguay, and Peru developed around a single primate city—Buenos Aires, Montevideo, and Lima, respectively—Colombia evolved toward a more polycentric urban structure. Three Andean cordilleras and river systems cross the country, making surface communication difficult and costly. Rather than a single dominant port-metropolis, Colombian growth produced multiple regional centers.

In the first half of the twentieth century, Barranquilla on the Caribbean coast emerged as the main gateway for foreign trade and immigration, while Bogota, Medellin, and Cali consolidated as inland nodes of administration, industry, and commerce. By the early 1950s, Colombia had around 11.5 million inhabitants; Bogota, the largest city, counted fewer than 700,000, followed by Medellin with more than 350,000, with rapidly growing centers such as Cali and Barranquilla. Department-level estimates of GDP per capita confirm this pattern: Bogota and Atlantico (Barranquilla) significantly exceeded the national average, Antioquia and Valle del Cauca were moderately above it, while many interior departments remained well below.[21]

Colombia's geography contrasts sharply with the urban structures of the nations from which El Dorado drew its talent. In Argentina, the 1947 census recorded a national population of 15.89 million, with nearly 20% concentrated in Buenos Aires. Peru, with a population of around 7.78 million in 1950, was increasingly dominated by its capital. Paraguay, though highly rural, was centered on Asunción (1950 pop: ~206,000), which served as the single, undisputed national pole. Brazil presented a bipolar model, with its two principal centers, Rio de Janeiro and São Paulo, acting as the dominant forces. The picture is more extreme in Uruguay, where by 1950, Montevideo was home to an estimated 68% of the nation's total population.

This polycentric urban system had significant social and cultural implications. It fostered strong regional identities that expressed themselves in politics, commerce, and everyday life. Economic competition between these regions coexisted with a shared national framework but also with mutual stereotypes and rivalries. Where Argentina's elite could imagine the nation primarily from Buenos Aires, Colombia's elites were distributed across at least four major urban poles, each with its own press, business associations, and cultural institutions.

Map 1.1 shows the distribution of cities that had a football club during El Dorado. It emphasizes the Andes mountain range and its division into three cordilleras (East, Central, and West) in the Southern part of the country. As of today, the country has been unable to dominate the mighty Andes, which in the 1950s led to the development of a relatively modern air travel industry.

Sport became an important channel for these regional competitors. During the 1930s, multisport events such as the *Juegos Deportivos Nacionales* and the Bolivarian Games required cities to build or upgrade stadiums and other facilities. In Barranquilla, the 1935 National Games stimulated the construction of a municipal stadium, the Romelio Martínez. In Manizales, the Palogrande stadium was built for the 1936 National Games and quickly became a symbol of the city's ambition within the coffee-growing region. In Bogota, the Nemesio Camacho "El Campín", inaugurated in 1938 during the first Bolivarian Games, stood as a central venue for football and athletics alike.[22]

These investments were not driven solely by football, but they created the physical infrastructure that professional clubs would later occupy. They also reinforced the association between cities and sporting excellence: departmental delegations competed to represent their regions. By the late 1940s, with the establishment of professional football, the rivalry between Antioquia (capital Medellin), Valle (Cali), Bogota, and the Caribbean coast (with Barranquilla as its flagship) was already familiar to the nation.

In comparative perspective, this territorial pattern helps explain why Colombia could sustain, for a few years, a national league with multiple strong clubs distributed across several cities. Unlike Uruguay, where Montevideo's

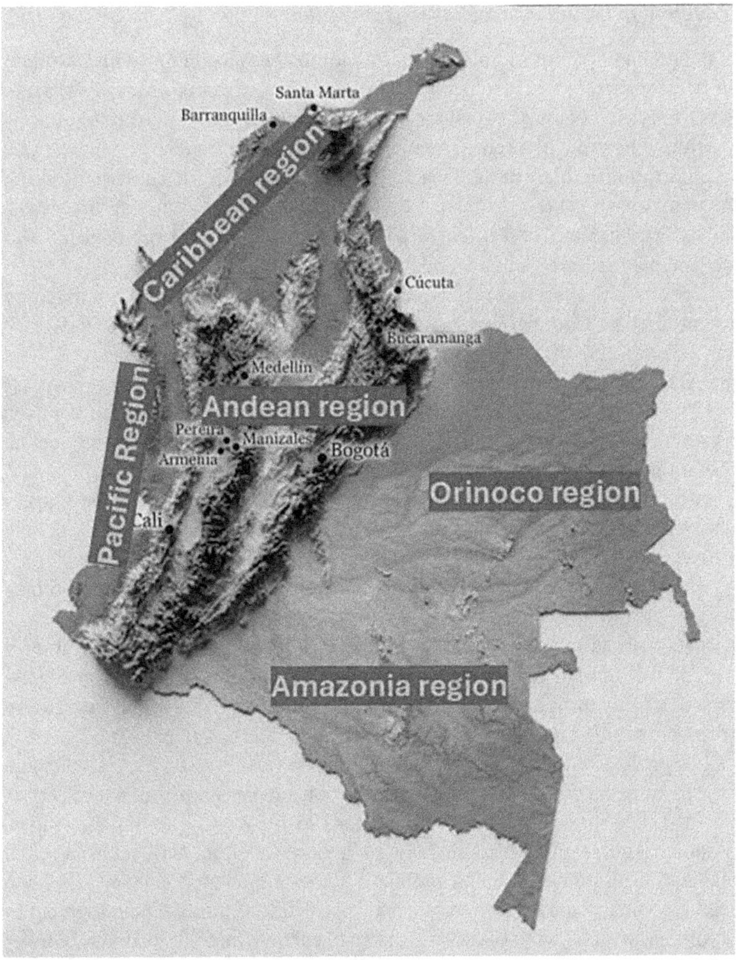


*Map 1.1* Spatial distribution of football cities

dominance concentrated the football system, or Peru, where Lima overshadowed other centers, Colombia's professional league could draw on clusters of fans, entrepreneurs, and media in several regional capitals.

At the same time, the same geography that favored regional differentiation made national integration costly—mountain ranges, poor roads, and fragmented railways limited mobility. For football, this meant that transforming regional rivalries into a coherent national league required not only stadiums, but also a transport technology capable of overcoming distance.

### *Overcoming the transport challenge: aviation*

In the realm of transport, mid-century Colombia was a country with a modern air fleet and an archaic land network. Road and rail systems, as it is still true in the twenty-first century, remained sparse, discontinuous, and of poor quality. Currie's report devoted considerable attention to the deficiencies of surface transport, noting high costs, long travel times, and the difficulties of linking the main urban centers with each other and with ports.[23] Railway lines were short, disconnected, and oriented primarily toward linking regional hubs to the Magdalena River.

Yet precisely because surface transport was so difficult, aviation assumed a central role. Commercial aviation in Colombia dates back to 1919 with the creation of the *Sociedad Colombo-Alemana de Transportes Aéreos* (SCADTA), which later merged with *Servicio Aéreo Colombiano* (SACO) in 1940, creating Avianca. By mid-century, the country possessed one of the densest domestic air networks in Latin America. It was not the only airline operating at the time. Between 1945 and 1954, *Líneas Aereas Nacional S.A.* (Lansa) competed with Avianca. Although the latter transported the players across the country, the former played a role by offering an alternative for the press and its reports to reach fans and enthusiasts in a timely manner.

Airlines already carried a large share of passenger traffic between Colombian cities and an increasing proportion of high-value freight, in many cases at costs comparable to or lower than those of road or river transportation.[24] For the Colombian economy, air transport enabled the coordination of dispersed administrative, commercial, and industrial centers and the integration of remote regions into national circuits of exchange.

For professional football, this infrastructure was fundamental. The league created in 1948 depended from its inception on the ability of clubs, referees, and, occasionally, journalists and fans to fly weekly across the Andes. Without regular flights connecting Bogota, Medellin, Cali, Barranquilla, Manizales, and other cities, a national, home-and-away league would have been logistically impossible. Airlines were a pillar of football development in Colombia, which had to overcome distance barriers that did not exist in other South American countries.

This dependence had several consequences. On the one hand, it allowed the league to operate at a genuinely national scale despite the country's fragmented geography. On the other hand, it added a layer of fixed costs to club finances. The same foreign-exchange flows that made high player salaries possible were also needed to pay for aviation fuel, maintenance, and airplane tickets on domestic routes. In a narrow window of time—roughly from 1949 to 1953—these conditions aligned. Coffee export revenues, industrial profits, and a stable currency financed both wages and intensive use of air travel. Regional elites seized the opportunity to demonstrate their city's modernity by recruiting international stars and flying them across the country, while radio stations turned these journeys into part of the spectacle, narrating not just the matches but the itineraries and arrivals of famous players.

The spatial fragmentation of Colombia was briefly turned into an asset for a modern national entertainment industry. But once again, this configuration was fragile. When the international coffee market turned less favorable, when import needs rose, and macroeconomic pressures intensified, when FIFA's sanctions restricted the recruitment of foreign players, and when domestic politics became more uncertain, the fixed costs of sustaining such a geographically stretched league became harder to bear. The very reliance on aviation that had made the national league possible also made it vulnerable to fluctuations in foreign-exchange availability and domestic credit.

### *Labor market and structural changes*

Viewing Colombia between 1948 and 1953 as a society in transition explains the extraordinary rise of El Dorado and its brevity. On the international side of the football labor market, economic volatility and state intervention in Argentina, the players' strike of 1948, and broader instability in other South American leagues created a pool of world-class players seeking more secure contracts abroad. On the Colombian side, coffee-driven export surpluses, a relatively stable exchange rate, and the growing wealth of regional (agro) industrial and commercial elites allowed clubs to offer salaries that, in dollar terms, were highly competitive.

On the domestic demand side, rapid urban population growth, the emergence of a new working and middle class, and the spread of radio created a market for modern spectacles, including professional football. The importance of radio in selling the myth of wonderful players scoring unimaginable goals should not be underestimated.

The radio not only transmitted the games but also created legends through programs like *El Trailer Futbolero*, where Carlos Arturo Rueda C., a pioneer in Colombia for "singing" a long goooaaall, narrated every goal from the weekend's fixtures. The program, broadcast at 8 p.m. on Sundays, had no video footage of the goals, so his narrations relied entirely on oral accounts—lending them an inevitable air of myth.[25]

Yet the Colombian market was constrained by low average incomes, high inequality, and persistent deficits in housing, health, and education. In that sense, El Dorado anticipated a future Colombia more than it reflected the Colombia of its time.

The league belonged to a potential society in which urban working and middle classes would be larger and more prosperous, public transport more developed, and mass entertainment more broadly affordable. The transitional nature of mid-century Colombia made it possible to stage such a league briefly, but also difficult to sustain it. Once coffee prices shifted, exchange-rate arrangements changed, international football authorities reasserted control over transfers, and domestic political and economic conditions tightened, the underlying limits of the social and economic base for professional football became apparent, and the exceptional moment of El Dorado drew to a close.

## Notes

1 See, among others, Goldblatt (2007, pp. 274–277).
2 Rougier and Stawski (2014), p. 29.
3 World Bank (1950), p. 2.
4 Kalmanovitz and López (2010).
5 Bértola and Ocampo (2012).
6 Kalmanovitz and López (2010).
7 Kalmanovitz and López (2010).
8 World Bank (1950).
9 Flórez (2000).
10 World Bank (1950).
11 Kalmanovitz and López (2010).
12 Kalmanovitz and López (2010).
13 World Bank (1950).
14 Kalmanovitz and López (2010).
15 Banco de la República (1998).
16 El Heraldo, July 2, 1949, p. 6.
17 El Heraldo, April 7, 1951, p. 9.
18 El Tiempo, July 8, 1949, p. 16.
19 El Tiempo, June 2, 1951, p. 9.
20 See, for instance, Walvin (1994); Mason (1980); Frydenberg (2011); Alabarces (2018); or Goldblatt (2007).
21 Kalmanovitz and López (2010).
22 Alcaldía Mayor de Bogota (2013).
23 World Bank (1950).
24 World Bank (1950).
25 Available ad about the program in El Tiempo, May 20, 1950, p. 21. and Mateus Nariño (2022) pp. 61–62.

## References

Alabarces, P. (2018). *Historia mínima del fútbol en América Latina*. El Colegio de Mexico AC.

Alcaldía Mayor de Bogota. (2013). *Estadio Nemesio Camacho El Campín*. Instituto Distrital de Patrimonio Cultural.

Banco de la República. (1998). Principales Indicadores Económicos. 1923–1997.

Bértola, Luis, and José Antonio Ocampo. (2012). *The Economic Development of Latin America since Independence*. Oxford University Press.

El Heraldo. Various Numbers. Archive Diario El Heraldo.

El Tiempo. Various Numbers. Available at https://news.google.com/newspapers?nid=N2osnxbUuuUC

Flórez, Carmen Elisa. (2000). *Las transformaciones sociodemográficas en Colombia*. Banco de la República—Tercer Mundo.

Frydenberg, Julio. (2011). *Historia social del fútbol: del amateurismo a la profesionalización*. Siglo XXI.

Goldblatt, D. (2007). *The ball is round: A global history of football*. Penguin UK.

Kalmanovitz, Salomón, and Edwin López. (2010). *Nueva historia económica de Colombia*. Taurus.

Londoño, Juan Luis. (1995). Distribución del ingreso y desarrollo económico: Colombia en el siglo XX. Banco de la República.

Nariño, Mateus. (2022). *Entre balones y pedales. Una mirada a la narración deportiva en Colombia.* Tesis de grado para Comunicador Social, Universidad Javeriana, Bogota. https://apidspace.javeriana.edu.co/server/api/core/bitstreams/8e21c0e2-b3f0-468b-9836-38ad92a88d7a/content

Mason, Tony. (1980). *Association Football and English Society, 1863–1915*. Harvester.

Rougier, M., and Stawski, M. (2014). Vientos de cambio. Las reformas administrativas y el Plan Económico de 1949. In Marcelo Rougier, Eduardo Gálvez, Patricia Jerez, Juan Odisio and Martín Stawski (eds.), *Perspectivas sobre la Industria 2: documento de trabajo* (pp. 7–32). Universidad de Buenos Aires, Facultad de Ciencias Económicas. CEEED.

Walvin, James. (1994). *The People's Game: The History of Football Revisited*. Mainstream.

World Bank. (1950). *The Basis of a Development Program for Colombia: Report of a Mission headed by Lauchlin Currie*. Washington, DC: International Bank for Reconstruction and Development.

# 2 Labor markets, piracy, and football

## Governance clash and the rise of piracy

By the late 1940s, Colombia was a society in transition. These conditions made a national league possible but not inevitable. To turn structural potential into a concrete competition, institutions were required, and those institutions were shaped by intense regional rivalries.

This chapter first reconstructs the long history of regionalism in Colombian football, from competing origin stories to the struggles over the headquarters and authority of the *Federación Colombiana de Fútbol* (Adefútbol). We then trace the emergence of professional football in the 1940s to the creation of Dimayor in 1948, and the sequence of conflicts that culminated in early 1949 with an institutional break: Dimayor's decision to ignore Adefútbol's authority and sign foreign players without transfer papers. That decision turned a domestic governance dispute into what the rest of the football world denounced as "pirate" professionalism. These were necessary conditions to "pull" players beyond Colombia's borders.

### *Regionalism*

Colombia's political and economic history is strongly shaped by regional differentiation. During the El Dorado years, the national economy and population were concentrated in the Andean and Caribbean regions: the former contained Bogota, Medellin, and Cali, while the latter revolved around Barranquilla, Cartagena, and Santa Marta.

Rivalries exist within regions—Antioquia versus Bogota being the most salient case—but the long-standing tension between the Caribbean and Andean regions has been particularly consequential for football governance. The Caribbean coast has historically been oriented toward migration networks, while the Andean interior developed around highland cities connected by difficult terrain. These differences shaped competing claims about football's origins and, later, conflicts over institutional authority and headquarters.

DOI: 10.4324/9781003396024-2

The clash initiated with the dawn of football in Colombia. While there is always room for debate over who introduced football to Latin America first, the story is relatively straightforward across most of the continent. Football, to Colombia, entered through Barranquilla. That is the answer of anyone born in the city and sustained in the official website of today's Colombian Football Association: "The most reliable argument is held by Barranquilla, upon beginning, in 1900, the construction of the railroad in Puerto Colombia".[1] Moreover, classic books tend to situate the birth of Colombian football in Barranquilla following Arturo de Castro's return from his education in Britain.[2] The year is not clear, though. While some mention that de Castro returned in 1908, others are more ambiguous and situate the first football match in 1904. Contemporary reports also note that Barranquilla is the door for football in Colombia. Humberto Salcedo Fernández wrote in 1950 that "the practice or activity of football had its origins in the City of Barranquilla in the year 1906".[3] Still, other versions state that football entered in 1909 via Santa Marta or Pasto.[4]

Years earlier, however, on July 21, 1882, *El Telegrama* from Bogota published the rules of football brought by the US Army Colonel Henry Rowan Lemly, who, as an advisor to the Military Academy, established this sport as part of their activities.[5] Following that event are reports of multiple football-related events in Bogota before 1904.[6] For people in the Caribbean region, the version that the origin of football in the country is not Barranquilla (or at least Santa Marta) is unacceptable.

The first national football league in Colombia was established in the 1920s, during the emergence of the "National Games", a multisport event that helped develop Olympism in the country. Football, attracting growing interest across regions, became part of these games. When the first National Games were held in Cali in 1928, football was included in the program.

Whatever its origins, football began its expansion across the country in a relatively unorganized manner. Not until 1920 were reports of a more thorough organization of the sport. That year, the government created the *Junta Central de Deportes*, the Central Sports Board, to organize football in the country. On July 28, a final was played in front of 2,000 people in Bogota. The game was significant enough to attract the former Colombian President, Rafael Reyes, and a member of the Spanish Royal Family, Jaime de Borbón.[7] Contemporary newspapers described the match as the final of the National Football Championship, but little is known of any sequels.

Over the following years, organized football spread, mainly within the four major cities. But it was Barranquilla that took a definitive step in founding the Colombian Association of Football on October 12, 1924, which initially served as the amateur football league.[8]

Intending to affiliate the newly formed League with CONMEBOL and FIFA, it initially applied for legal recognition from the Colombian government, which was granted by resolution 34 of 1927.[9] The resolution forced future regional leagues to abide by the Football League, which they promoted by sending emissaries across the country to create regional leagues that should join them by their rules.[10]

The next step was to request that the government officially recognize the Football League as the Colombian Football Association. Following Carlos Lafaurie Roncallo's request as President of the Football League, President Alfonso López granted it on resolution number 72 of 1936.[11] Adefútbol then applied for admission to CONMEBOL and FIFA, which granted the request later that year. Importantly, throughout this process, it was clear that Adefútbol's headquarters were in Barranquilla.

However, regionalism would gain momentum as early as 1938. Barranquilla was proposing that member clubs themselves fund Adefútbol, prompting objections from Antioquia that the Association would lack the moral authority to sanction any of its financial backers. Antioquia subsequently requested a separation between the *Liga del Atlántico*, the regional football league, and the national league.[12]

Eventually, Antioquia secured a decision by the National Commission for Physical Education to revoke Adefútbol's legal status as a first step toward relocating its headquarters to Medellin. Adefútbol's strategy was to secure support from all its affiliates and, beginning a ritual it would maintain for years, wrote to CONMEBOL and FIFA to defend them as the legal representative of Colombian football. CONMEBOL and FIFA recognized Adefútbol as the rightful head of Colombian football, leading to an agreement in which, again in 1939, the government granted it official recognition as the country's leading football institution.[13]

In December 1938, however, the government issued Decree 2216, which recognized only one Association per sport and granted Barranquilla the football headquarters.[14] The regulation was later revised on July 5, 1939, which restored a formal role for general assemblies in deciding the headquarters every four years and introduced a procedure for intervention by the National Commission for Physical Education when affiliated leagues alleged that an association was acting against the interests of the sport.[15]

By 1944, Adefútbol had to organize national meetings to present the Association's situation to its affiliates and, if required, to vote on the location of the headquarters. However, Efraín Borrero, president of Adefútbol, unilaterally canceled the meeting in July.[16] Under criticisms that Barranquilla did little to expand the sport, that there was no consistent representation of Colombia in international tournaments, and with the upcoming 1945 South American Football Championship in Chile in sight, the meeting took place in October.

At this point, the discussion was intense between the representatives of the football leagues of Antioquia, Valle, Cundinamarca (whose capital at the time was Bogota), and Choco, and Adefútbol's President Efraín Borrero, who, according to the former, focused on the defense of Barranquilla as the home of the Association but did little to promote the sport.[17]

The meeting voted for a new headquarters, with Medellin narrowly losing to Barranquilla by five votes to four.[18] The losing delegates requested that the Colombian Olympic Committee (COC) and the Ministry of Education reconsider the results. The COC, in a meeting in Bogota with the delegates from Barranquilla absent, conceded the headquarters to Medellin.[19] Thus, Colombia had two football associations, one in Barranquilla and another in Medellin.

By December 1944, Colombia was simultaneously announcing that there would be (Medellin) and would not be (Barranquilla) a Colombian national team in Chile.[20] Ultimately, a national team composed of players from Barranquilla, Santa Marta, and Caldas represented the country at the tournament in Chile. Colombia conceded 25 goals in six games, finishing only above Ecuador and Bolivia.

Barranquilla, though, did win. CONMEBOL defended Adefútbol as the unique legitimate representative of Colombia to FIFA and advocated for the unification of its football.[21] The division was structural. Thus, if Adefútbol organized, the leagues would not obey; if the leagues planned, Adefútbol would not authorize.[22] The need for another vision, a professional approach to the sport, became necessary.

The country was prepared for more, and beyond flying for friendlies across the country, clubs from Argentina, Brazil, Ecuador, Paraguay, Peru, and Uruguay came to Colombia. Thus, by March 1948, Adefútbol was preparing a draft for a new professional football competition. Since Deportivo Municipal (the predecessor of Millonarios) began importing foreign players, Colombian players complained that they were not receiving payments. Indeed, Municipal started to be called the "club of the rich". It evolved into Millionaires (*Millonarios* in Spanish), and the name was adopted when it registered as a limited company in 1946. Thus, the team began paying for games won, among other bonuses. It gave birth to the so-called "brown professionalism".[23]

On June 9, Adefútbol convened its affiliated leagues and interested clubs for a General Assembly on June 26 to draft the constitution of the Major League—a body that, under Adefútbol's authority, would assume governance of professional football in Colombia.[24] In late June in Barranquilla, after intense debate, Adefútbol agreed to create the professional *Liga Mayor de Fútbol,* "Major Football League"*, with 11* teams. With the opposition of the *Liga del Atlántico*, four teams from Antioquia (Victoria, Huracán, Atlético Municipal, Medellín), two from Valle (América, Deportivo Cali), two from Manizales (Deportes Caldas, Once Deportivo), two from Bogota (Millonarios, Santa Fe), and Junior of Barranquilla agreed to start a new professional tournament later in August that year.[25] The *Liga Major* (also known as *División Mayor No Amateur*—non-amateur major division and eventually Dimayor), with headquarters in Bogota, named Humberto Salcedo Fernández as its first President, would be independent of amateur football and would provisionally be affiliated with Adefútbol. The agreement included that amateur leagues would receive 5% of gross attendance revenue when they played the preliminary match of a professional game, but nothing if they did not play.[26] The Barranquilla newspaper—El Heraldo—wrote about locating Dimayor's headquarters in Bogota, "that represents a stab in the back to local football and the effort made over many years by the pioneers of this sport in Barranquilla"—regionalism at work.[27] Thus, the debate was less about the importance of opening a football league and more about who would control the professional league and its expected revenues.

In Barranquilla, there were concerns about Adefútbol's capacity to rule over the nascent Dimayor. "Domestic football has new owners and a new Zar who is giving categorical orders, and those orders must be obeyed", wrote in July 1948 El Heraldo.[28]

With ups and downs and limiting it to only two teams per city, professional football began on August 15, 1948. Supported by Avianca, Millonarios, Santa Fe from Bogota, Junior from Barranquilla, América, Deportivo Cali from Cali, Atlético Municipal and Medellín from Medellin, Once Deportivo and Deportes Caldas from Manizales, and Universidad, originally from Bogota, but forced to play in Pereira, composed the first professional national league in the country.

### *The pull*

The history of El Dorado is rich in myths that do not necessarily align with actual events. In "Ball is Round", Goldblatt states that football was part of the conservatives' government scheme to provide a circus to the people, helping keep them under control after the events of *El Bogotazo*, and that Dimayor was disaffiliated from FIFA. It also states that the opening games, scheduled for May 1948, were delayed until August.[29]

In his book on Argentine football, Jonathan Wilson cites a source stating that "soccer was the only thing that the government could think of to control and calm the population after the death of Gaitán".[30] The source is Carl Worswick, a British journalist specializing in Colombian football, who interviews Guillermo Ruíz Bonilla, whom he describes as the "most respected football historian" in Colombia.[31] In that interview, Ruíz Bonilla defends the claim that the government directly supported the idea of a national league. Moreover, he defends that Alfonso Senior personally told him that without Gaitán's death, "the start of the league in Colombia would have been delayed by years".[32]

There is no evidence of this. The contemporary press explicitly acknowledges that professional football in Colombia "began amid official indifference. Without help, but without direct attacks".[33] As far as our research goes, the idea that professional football arose due to *El Bogotazo* and the government's need to offer a spectacle to the people is nothing but a myth.

A working idea of a professional football league dates back, at least to mid-1947, when, in a meeting in Barranquilla, Adefútbol proposed a regional league seeking control of the tournament.[34] The project did not prosper, but a draft was circulating in March 1948, before Gaitán's assassination. The success of Vélez Sarsfield's (Argentina) and River Plate's (Uruguay) matches against Millonarios and Santa Fe in Bogota in early 1948 was a decisive push for the creation of the league.

Despite the absence of professional football, Santa Fe and Millonarios invested in foreign players. Santa Fe brought several players from the national team that played in the 1947 South American Championship. Millonarios, meanwhile, had in its roster players such as Alfredo Castillo (Argentine), and Uruguayans Alcides Aguilera, and José Saule.[35]

There is no tangible evidence that the government was directly interested in a professional league following *El Bogotazo*. It is probably true that organized football could be a "good painkiller to help people forget the pain", giving sense to Senior's words to Ruíz Bonilla.[36]

The absence of official interest in the professional league became evident when the conservative Governor of Antioquia, Arango Ferrer, appointed by the President on April 10, 1948, just one day after *El Bogotazo,* designated the board members of the regional league. Expressing dissatisfaction with the technical, and administrative aspects of Adefútbol and Dimayor, the Antioquia League summoned the other leagues to dissolve the former and create a new one.[37]

With the professional league in motion, the Antioquia League complained that the professional teams were not affiliated with it. In a daring move, the Governor of Antioquia, Arango Ferrer, threatened to ban the game between Municipal and Deportes Caldas if Municipal did not pay the corresponding fee. Atlético Municipal paid, but Medellín did not pay a week later. Hence, the governor canceled the October 3, 1948, game between Medellín and Santa Fe. Upon the threat of canceling football matches in Medellin, son enough, on October 8, the Antioquia Football League, in meetings held in Dimayor's offices in Bogota, agreed to recognize and abide by Adefútbol rules.[38]

Adefútbol and Dimayor were not challenged only by Antioquia but had problems of their own. A month earlier, in September, Adefútbol and Dimayor had broken relations because the latter would not accept the former's adjustment of its statutes. The amateur leagues sought to control amateur and professional football. Adefútbol sought to limit the number of foreign players to five, which would immediately leave six of the ten teams unable to compete. Moreover, they were also requesting the five percent fee and demanded a 50% discount on match tickets for league-affiliated supporters.[39] Dimayor issued a resolution directing that the 2% fee that professional clubs had been paying to Adefútbol be deposited into a special account, while the 5% owed to amateur leagues be earmarked for promoting amateur competitions and matches.[40]

In the first of many reconciliations, Dimayor agreed to have, "in most games", a preliminary match between amateur teams affiliated with the leagues recognized by Adefútbol. On the Antioquia matter, both decided that Adefútbol would unify the norms in the election process to avoid politicians naming the leagues' boards. At the same time, Antioquia accepted the role of Dimayor in Adefútbol.[41] Adefútbol decided to "provisionally" affiliate again with Dimayor.[42] The 2% of gross revenue would go to Adefútbol, and the 5% to the amateur leagues.[43]

As the first edition of the professional league ended and with the 1949 South American Football Championship in sight, Adefútbol was torn internally. Adefútbol appointed Ezequiel Díaz Granados, a highly reputed Barranquilla officer, as its president on September 15, 1948. He resigned with a letter dated November 9, accusing the Atlantic Football League of being an obstacle to bringing together Adefútbol and Dimayor. He further alleged that delegates from Cundinamarca, Valle, and Magdalena had passed resolutions in the Board during his absence.[44] Indeed, by the end of 1948, Adefútbol was still trying to figure out how to reform its statutes to accommodate Dimayor and its professional league.

At the dawn of 1949, professional teams organized several international friendlies. Adefútbol threatened to refuse to authorize Universidad de Lima (Peru) and Madureira (Brazil) to play in Bogota against Santa Fe and Millonarios because Dimayor had not paid the corresponding percentages for the 1948 tournament. Quickly enough, both teams made the corresponding payments, allowing Universidad to play in Colombia.

A relevant matter for Adefútbol was Colombia's participation in the South American Championship, expected to take place in March in Rio de Janeiro (Brazil). In January 1949, Adefútbol offered the manager position to the Argentine Fernando Paternoster, coach of Atlético Municipal (Medellin). In the January Dimayor meeting, the professional teams agreed to pay the COP 20,000 (USD 10,204) that Adefútbol requested to send the National team, using part of the 2% that Adefútbol would receive from the 1949 football league.[45]

Despite Dimayor's intentions, by mid-February 1949, they had only COP15,000 (USD 7,653), funded by Santa Fe, Millonarios, the Cundinamarca Football League, and teams from Cali and Medellin. Dimayor suggested that Adefútbol loan the remaining COP 5,000 (USD 2,551), since Dimayor still lacked legal status and therefore could not receive such a sum directly.[46]

Dimayor approved Proposition No. 2, which sought guarantees for the funds to be delivered. From Dimayor's point of view, the proposition was a statement to professionalize the National team's participation in the event while bringing them to the level of Adefútbol. Thus, in its first point, the proposition declared that a representative of Dimayor and a representative of Adefútbol would jointly select the delegation. The second point, which probably most offended Adefútbol, required Adefútbol to provide verified accounts of the expenses incurred by the delegation. The last point stated that Dimayor would repay the COP5,000 loan made by Adefútbol, plus the 2% fee from the 1949 tournament.

On the afternoon of February 23, 1949, a radiogram from Adefútbol to Dimayor stated their disappointment, accusing Dimayor of impeding Colombia's participation in the South American Championship. The message concluded with Adefútbol noting that they would inform CONMEBOL.[47]

Almost immediately, on the evening of the 23rd, Dimayor replied with another radiogram, maintaining that they had honored their commitments and accepting the decision not to travel to Rio. Dimayor added that it would finance Adefútbol's trip to Brazil to secure Colombia's hosting rights for the 1951 South American Championship, which had previously been awarded to the country.[48]

Adefútbol reacted in the worst possible way, which given the dates, suggests a response prepared since Dimayor's Proposition No. 2. Dated February 21, 1949, but announced the 23rd, Adefútbol issued its Resolution No. 3 canceling the ongoing tours of foreign clubs in Colombia including Madureira (Brazil), Universidad (Peru), Sporting Tabaco (Perú), Deportivo Municipal (Peru), and Alianza (Peru).[49] It turned out, however, that there was no legal quorum when adopting Resolution No. 3 as Mario Abello, Régulo Matera, and Mario J. Márquez, members of Adefútbol representing the professional league, were not invited to the meeting. Clubs like Millonarios and Santa Fe had invested heavily and risked lawsuits for breach of contract.[50]

On the 24th, Adefútbol issued Proposition No. 1, denouncing Dimayor's Proposition No. 2 as disrespectful and rejecting Dimayor's assistance if it came at the cost of its jurisdictional authority.[51] Humberto Salcedo Fernández, President of Dimayor, wanted to break ties with Adefútbol.[52] Indeed, Dimayor ignored Adefútbol's Resolution No. 3, as no matches were canceled. Adefútbol lost support. Even the Barranquilla press was confused, noting that "resolution No. 3 was born from a moment of clouded judgment due to financial disagreements. We cannot take their side because we believe an almost omnipotent institution like Adefútbol must carry itself with gravitas when issuing its rulings".[53]

With no support, Adefútbol backed down, revoking Resolution No. 3 on March 4. Simultaneously, they issued Resolution No. 4, which selected a national team to send to Brazil, composed of 12 Junior players: 5 from Medellín, 1 from Santa Marta, and the Santa Fe goalkeeper, "Chonto" Gaviria.[54] It was hardly a Colombian national team, but a Barranquilla team representing Colombia.

Among the travelers to Brazil, Adefútbol announced Mario Abello and Regulo Matera, representatives of Dimayor. Dimayor replied swiftly on March 9, 1949: not only did they ban all professional players from flying to Brazil, but they also threatened to disaffiliate any club for three years and any player for two years who decided to attend Adefútbol's invitation. Abello and Matera were ousted from Dimayor's board. Adefútbol counterattacked. It disaffiliated Dimayor and banned senior officials based in Bogota.[55] Total rupture.

Junior decided to unconditionally back Adefútbol. Meanwhile, in Bogota, the COC, which by law had the right to authorize trips abroad, denied such approval. Moreover, it requested that the Foreign Ministry deny the necessary visas to visit Brazil.[56]

The first quarter of 1949 ended with Dimayor disaffiliated from Adefútbol, Junior expelled from Dimayor for three years, numerous players suspended for two years, and a Colombian national team composed mainly of Junior players *en route* to Brazil. The Medellín players and "Chonto" Gaviria decided to avoid any sanctions and withdrew from the team. Mario Abello, expelled from Dimayor, accepted a position as Junior's managing director. Colombia finished last in the South American tournament.

At the Congress following the South American Championship, Adefútbol managed to get CONMEBOL to disregard Dimayor's authority. Dimayor responded in early May 1949. It decided not to accept any international jurisdiction from any organization, to eliminate the payment of any revenue percentages to Adefútbol and the amateur leagues, and to open the door for foreign players to join the league freely. With the 2% previously paid to Adefútbol, Dimayor agreed to import foreign referees to improve the quality of the league.[57] The door toward El Dorado was now wide open. Piracy would loom over the landscape for the foreseeable future.

Upon returning from Rio, Bernardo Jaramillo García, Adefútbol's President, warned that any foreign players in Colombia would be disqualified. Moreover, he vowed to limit the number of foreign players, none within a year.[58] His attitude contrasts with Dimayor's, which still defended Adefútbol as the representative of Colombian football but called for changes in the Association's managerial strategies.[59]

Still, in mid-June 1949, Adefútbol and Dimayor were seemingly negotiating a truth. The draft agreement called for Dimayor to reaffiliate Junior, settle its debts to Adefútbol and the amateur leagues, and recognize Adefútbol as the arbiter of any disputes in professional football. All efforts were in vain. Pedernera was already in Colombia. He and El Dorado arrived on June 10, 1949.

A few months later, in October 1949, following claims that Colombia had hired footballers without transfer papers, FIFA sent a message expelling Dimayor. The Colombian response was as true as it was arrogant: "Dimayor has never been affiliated with FIFA, thus it cannot be expelled from where it does not belong".[60] The consequences were that no club affiliated to FIFA could play against a Dimayor team unless authorized by Adefútbol.

## The push: why did the best come to Colombia?

A significant number of foreign players came to Colombia, driven by circumstances in their home countries. The specifics of Argentina, Brazil, England, Hungary, Paraguay, Peru, and Uruguay explain much of why so many joined what became history's first globalized football league.

### *Argentina*

Argentine players were in Colombia even before the country had a professional football league. Three, for instance, played for Millonarios in 1947: Paratore, Castillo, and Cabillón. However, they were not the high-quality players who would follow Pedernera's footsteps. Indeed, the name of Adolfo Pedernera is key to El Dorado, not only because he was the first to arrive but also primarily because of his significance for Argentine football: he was the "Maestro", the Master, the "greatest player of the modern era".[61] *El Gráfico* magazine, more poetically, wrote: "In the game where the ball should be everything, he made the ball a secondary thing".[62]

Argentine footballers, winners of the South American championships of 1945, 1946, and 1947, were among the first to push for better working conditions. As soon as the last quarter of 1945, the players were trying to negotiate the employment regime with the Argentine Football Association (AFA). Though not always openly supportive of the Peronist administration, the Union never broke ties with it. In 1946, following a meeting with President Perón, the organization successfully registered *Futbolistas Argentinos Agremiados* (FAA). That, however, was just the first step toward recognition of the union.[63]

Three were the key petitions that the Union pushed for. They wanted recognition from both the government and AFA as a crucial milestone in compelling clubs to acknowledge that playing football constituted a legitimate profession like any other. The other requests relate to the type of contractual regime. The players sought to eliminate the salary cap and to allow players to choose their destination when they become free agents. In line with tradition and FIFA's rules, clubs could retain a player even without a contract and against his will.

During the 1948 preseason, the FAA threatened to strike after making no progress in their petitions. In April, the AFA averted the strike when they recognized the Union as an official negotiating partner. The Union subsequently reached an agreement with Oscar L. Nicolini, the AFA President, in May 1948—a central figure in subsequent events.

The agreement represented a victory for the FAA, replacing the existing ARS1,500 (USD 373) monthly salary cap with a tiered minimum wage system. This new structure accounted for players' experience and club history, establishing monthly salaries ranging from ARS500 (USD 124) to ARS1,500.[64] The draft also stated that a player would be a free agent upon finishing his contract. According to Oscar Basso, the Union's president in July 1948, Nicolini surprisingly introduced the latter.[65] Furthermore, the agreement stipulated that free agents receiving domestic offers below ARS1,000 (USD 249) could negotiate with foreign teams without requiring a transfer pass.[66] The conflict appeared to be short-lived. Merely illusions.

Under a prevailing sentiment that clubs needed to "defend football, not the players", they remained reluctant to approve the agreement. The expectation was that the AFA's executive board would debate the accord by late May 1948. However, unable to reach a consensus, the board transferred the responsibility to the clubs' Presidents. Since neither AFA nor the clubs had approved the agreement, the FAA declared on June 28, 1948, that its members would boycott all matches until AFA's general assembly granted official approval. In response, the clubs issued a formal telegram to each player, attempting to circumvent the Union's authority:

"For the purpose of taking appropriate disciplinary and legal measures, please inform us within 24 hours if you will be part of the team next Sunday. Lack of response will be considered as a negative answer. Reply paid".[67] Many players, individually but in accordance with a collective agreement, replied to the telegram: "We endorse the decision of the Argentine Footballers Union".[68]

An atmosphere of deep suspicion pervaded the negotiations, with each party interpreting every statement through their lens of mistrust. Even Nicolini's legitimacy, respected by both parties, was a subject of debate. For instance, an AFA president's statement sparked further controversy when the Union interpreted his words as a direct proposal for a seven-day suspension of the strike. The AFA, however, vehemently disputed this interpretation, insisting that he had merely expressed confidence that if the players lifted the strike, seven days would be sufficient to resolve the underlying issues—not that he was advocating for a temporary pause.[69] The dispute concluded with the cancellation of matchday 12 of the Argentine professional league and AFA's suspension of all professional activities.

Negotiations stalled. The players needed a pronouncement for the assembly to discuss the possibility of lifting the strike. The clubs refused to negotiate with the strike still ongoing.

Peronism played a pivotal role in late-1940s Argentina, with Perón rising to power largely through labor union support. Despite this prolabor stance, significant debate remained about whether professional footballers were ordinary workers entitled to the same protections and benefits. This tension highlighted the unique position of athletes within the Peronist labor framework. Nicolini embodied this complex intersection of sports and politics, serving simultaneously as a high-ranking official within the Peronist bureaucracy and as president of the AFA.

Thus, probably not by chance, on July 9, Nicolini and the Minister of Finance, Cereijo, met at the *Teatro Colón* in Buenos Aires while enjoying a gala performance. The minister, aware of the situation, committed to intervene in the conflict, suggesting that the Peron government was feeling the strike and preferred the public on the stadium stands. The following day, July 10, 1948, Minister Cerijo summoned the union to his office at 10 a.m. to break the deadlock in negotiations.[70] Late that afternoon, the FAA and the AFA reached a breakthrough agreement, ending both the strike and championship suspension. The compromise established joint committees with extensive authority to examine each point in the players' list of demands, with one key exception: the free agency issue would require formal assembly approval from the AFA and the FAA. Both sides expressed confidence in closing an agreement within 15 days.

AFA and FAA reached a final agreement in mid-August 1948, satisfying the requests for free agency. Starting December 15, 1951, players would become free agents. Beginning in the 1949 season, salaries would increase by 15%–40%, effectively dropping the salary cap. The agreement also included safeguards against breaches. Any club failing to implement the mandated salary increases would automatically grant the affected player free-agent status. Conversely, players receiving the approved wage adjustments would be bound to their clubs under three-year contracts.[71] The agreement preserved the arbitration tribunal established in the original May accord. The tribunal's composition was explicitly structured: two AFA members, two FAA members, and one neutral representative collectively empowered to resolve any dispute.

The parties finally signed the August agreement in October 1948. The accord, overseen by Minister Cereijo, marked a significant victory for the players' labor movement. All that remained was for individual clubs to implement the terms they had collectively agreed upon.

The agreement between the FAA and AFA implied non-negligible compensation requirements. Thus, while the Union's assembly unanimously approved it in October, the clubs questioned their ability to comply with these new requirements, even as they faced increased obligations as the arbitration tribunal reviewed and sanctioned cases against them.

Whether the clubs were financially constrained or not, the Union claimed that 18 of 25 clubs were not paying.[72] On October 31, to pressure compliance, it ordered its members to stop playing for one minute in each game. AFA felt insulted and reacted harshly. Initially, the AFA board threatened to terminate the championship. However, within days, they proposed a more drastic solution: abolishing professional status and reverting to amateur football after 17 years of professionalism. Carlos Paillot, the President of Racing, disagreed: "It is necessary to act decisively to keep the work of 17 years of professionalism, where both leaders and players have given their best to football. Therefore, if we were to return to amateurism, it would be taking a step backward, and everything conquered until now, which is substantial, would have no value".[73]

This time, not only the finance minister got involved in the negotiations. With the backing of Army Major Carlos Aloé, Executive Secretary to President Perón, they persuaded the Union to issue a statement clarifying that the one-minute strike was not intended as defiance toward the AFA. The clubs, however, refused to attend the government's invitation to negotiate. On November 14, 1948, with a weak attendance, the games took place, but not with the professional squads.

Preparing for the judicial battle, the clubs had cited their players to play their respective games. Each club summoned notary officers to create a document recording their absence. The AFA board suspended the contracts of the striking players, banning them from training, leading to the termination of over 500 contracts.[74] AFA's decision carried a two-year suspension penalty, which terminated all payment obligations. However, except for Estudiantes de la Plata, which had settled its debts before terminating contracts, every club owed players Christmas bonuses and other payments—a situation that legally undermined their contract terminations. Indeed, as Di Stéfano recalls, the "problem was that the small teams would pay their players for the first two months, then the team wouldn't function properly, and they would stop paying". [75] Still, the clubs canceled salary payments and, having no professionals to pay, reduced ticket prices from ARS 1 to 80 cents (USD 0.21 to 0.16). [76]

With negotiations at an impasse, the parties turned to an arbitration body, the *Secretaría de Trabajo y Previsión* (Secretariat of Labor and Social Welfare). However, the Secretariat could only intervene on the condition that no strike was in progress. As a concession to end any job action, the Secretariat would formally recognize the Argentine Footballers' Union.

On November 20, the Union called off the strike.[77] While the government agency studied the labor conflict, the players remained contractless, and the AFA drafted new professional football regulations. A January 1949 draft included free agency upon contract expiration, and a controversial formula for payment. It stated that the players would receive 80% of matchday net revenues. Of this amount, 30% would go to first-division players as salary, 20% to reserve or academy players, and 30% to bonuses distributed among players or at the club's discretion.[78]

The formula did not add up. Considering gross, rather than net, revenues, the 80% for a big club like River Plate amounted to ARS 444,846 (USD 92,483) in 1948.[79] Dedicating 60% of that to salaries (adding the amounts devoted to salaries and bonuses) and assuming a roster of 22 players, the average monthly payment would add up to just over ARS 1,200 (USD 250). Recalling that the examples use gross rather than net, thereby biasing upward the players' final income, a footballer from a small club like Tigre would receive, on average, around ARS 560 (USD 116). To put the figures in perspective, Di Stéfano signed his first contract in 1946 for an annual fee of ARS 5000 (USD 1,040) and an ARS 600 (USD 125) monthly salary.[80] A couple of years later, his expectations were five times that amount.

The clubs, competing for talent, had steadily increased player compensation through under-the-table payments. Despite the salary cap of ARS 1,500 (USD 311), it was common knowledge that the stars received figures above it. During the strike, an anonymous player stated, "My club's finances can't be that bad if, instead of the regulatory $1,500, they're paying me $4,000 (USD 831)".[81] A young Di Stéfano is another example. At the start of the 1948 season, he refused to play until he signed his contract with River Plate, which he did for ARS 3,500 (USD 868), well above the salary cap.[82]

The annual fee necessary to lure the best players was initially capped at ARS 1,500 per year by mutual agreement, but the clubs covertly breached this ceiling, raising it to circa ARS 3,000. When they later increased the official cap to ARS 5,000 (USD 1,500), the pattern repeated, with certain clubs offering as much as ARS 8,000 (USD 1,649). [83]

Throughout early 1949, the AFA and its member clubs engaged in intense negotiations over player compensation. During meetings in late January, River Plate's influential president, Antonio Vespucio Liberti, proposed establishing a minimum wage between 300 and 500 Argentine pesos (USD 62–104) —significantly below the figures previously offered in the May 1948 agreement, which had established minimum wages ranging from 500 to 800 (USD 124–199) and up to 1,250 Argentine pesos (USD 311), depending on a player's tenure with their club and division level.[84] This proposal faced immediate opposition from smaller clubs.[85]

The conflict remained stagnant during the first two months of 1949, forcing AFA to delay the championship's start until the last week of April. Meanwhile, the Union decided that its members should not train, but by March some restarted to train. As Basso, the Union leader, pointed out, the players expected AFA to recognize the Union—initially achieved months earlier—and legalize the contracts.[86] River Plate offered to renew the contracts because, under AFA's provisions, suspended players would be reinstated. Following the Union's decision, the players rejected the offer.[87]

By April 1949, AFA made a pivotal move by issuing a new Contract Regime. It followed the January draft closely. However, it dismissed the minimum wage and reinstated the salary cap of ARS 1,500 plus ARS 150 per point earned.[88] Amadeo Carrizo, then 22 and later a legend for River Plate, was among the first to accept the new conditions.[89] Others followed, but most restrained themselves. However, the players identified some positive points, leading them to accept an arbitration tribunal to handle contract terminations in which AFA could exercise the presidency, at least while Nicolini was president.[90]

A crucial issue concerned the percentages assigned to pay players' salaries. Those from the small clubs complained that their wages, based on matchday revenues, would be as low as ARS 300 (USD 62) per month or even negative.[91] In contrast, some stars would not settle for less than ARS 3,000 (USD 622) a month. Rossi and Lostau, both from River Plate, expected ARS 3,500 (USD 728), while Di Stéfano would accept ARS 3,000. The latter was also acceptable for stars like Boyé (Boca Juniors), Pontoni (San Lorenzo), Pedernera (Huracán), and Julio Cozzi (Platense).[92]

At this point, the clubs got tougher. In April, River Plate summoned its players to either accept the contracts or be excluded from the professional squad for the 1949 tournament, suspended for two years, and banned from football in Argentina and every other country.[93]

The 1949 season started on April 26 despite most players refusing to sign their contracts. Nevertheless, the conflicting parties appeared to be moving toward resolution. Nicolini informed the Union that players' salaries would no longer be tied to match attendance, and that second-division players would be guaranteed a minimum wage of ARS 100 (USD 21).[94]

On April 26, the Union agreed to sign the deal—an agreement that could have been reached weeks earlier, given the preexisting salary cap. While this officially ended the strike, underlying tensions persisted as several star players remained dissatisfied with their compensation offers. River Plate players, for instance, Rossi, Ferrari, Coll, and Di Stéfano, signed the contract, almost under coercion, because "it was the last day, it was midnight, or we would be out of football".[95]

The Union signed, the strike ended, but the players, particularly the stars, resented the deal. The role of the union reveals a complex duality. In addition to the Union's recognition, the FAA's struggle helped make the unfair labor conditions visible. On the other hand, the consequence of the signed agreements weakened the very industry they wanted to improve. Beyond recognition and even considering the player's natural fatigue and increasing financial difficulties following six months of strike, working conditions did not change substantially from what they had been at the beginning of the conflict. Regarding the salary cap, they seemed to be in a worse position. The clubs, moreover, retained their right to decide the player's fate, even without a signed contract. Di Stéfano, who had had a contract above the salary cap, recognized that "after the strike, every player had a capped salary".[96]

The Colombian adventure began with the most significant historical figure without a contract: Adolfo Pedernera. At 30 years old, he played for Huracán, which he joined in 1948. Unlike other teammates, the club did not summon him to sign the contract. It is easy to speculate that his role in the Union played a part. Although Oscar Basso, who left for Italy, was the FAA's voice during the meetings, Adolfo Pedernera was also a significant figure in the negotiations.

At the outset of the strike, following Arnaldo Vásquez's petition, Pedernera requested the expulsion of those who defied the collective decision to strike. Basso managed to stall that proposal. Later, as the strike endangered Argentina's participation in the 1949 South American Championship in Brazil, Pedernera and Boyé led the decision to deny the national team from playing while the strike was ongoing.

With no contract, Pedernera, feeling that his football days were not over, considered: "Huracán can negotiate my transfer, setting a price. If they do not accept any offers, they must sign me under the same conditions as last year".[97]

Making just ARS 1,500 (USD 311), Boyé, Di Stéfano, and many other players received substantial international offers. However, their clubs were reluctant to sell. The exodus began slowly, with some star players moving to

FIFA-ruled countries in line with existing regulations. Boyé left for Italy, to Genova, for the ARS 280,000 (USD 58,212). Oscar Basso, the Union's leader, followed suit.[98]

Pedernera, with no clear options in Argentina, accepted Millonarios' offer despite playing in a league unaffiliated with FIFA. On June 7, 1949, Adolfo Pedernera, whom *Goles* magazine called the "genius of those who bloom only by exception", left Buenos Aires, giving birth to El Dorado.[99]

### *Peru*

Before Pedernera flew to Bogota, some Peruvian stars were arriving in Colombia, taking advantage of the Peruvian league's nonprofessional status. Indeed, a non-amateur Association was established in 1940, but it was not until 1951, pushed by the exodus to Colombia, that the Central Football Association organized the first professional league.[100]

In preparation for the South American 1949 championship, the Peruvian team concentrated in a military base. On Saturday, February 26, 1949, Valeriano López, the Peruvian superstar, Felix Mina, Juan Lecca, Juan Castillo, René Rosasco, and Eliseo Morales decided to party and escaped from *Las Palmas* military base.[101] Unfortunately for them, they were not stealthy enough. The consequences were as harsh as they could be. They were all expelled from the National team and disqualified from playing professional football.

During the 1949 preseason, four Peruvian teams toured Colombia. Universidad, Municipal, Sporting Tabaco, and Alianza. Their performance, winning eight and drawing three games out of 14 against Colombian teams, convinced Deportivo Cali to send Libardo Rivera Gómez, its General Director, to Peru. It is interesting to note that by May 1949, Colombian teams had already set their sights on the best Peruvian players. Rivera Gómez told the Peruvian press that "the way things are going, I believe it is not too optimistic to say that within two years we will be able to sign professional football stars from the Río de la Plata like Moreno, Labruna, Boyé".[102] Ironically, although Moreno arrived at Independiente Medellín in 1954, neither of these three players played in Colombia during *El Dorado*. Still, just a month later, the best of the best would start landing in Bogota.

Two reasons led Peruvians to move to Colombia. First, although they had contracts, their salaries at home were much lower. Second, there is evidence that, unlike in Argentina or Uruguay, Peruvian players became free agents when finishing their contracts. Indeed, in a May 1949 interview, Alfredo Mosquera, who already had an "interesting offer from Colombia", said that my contract "expires this year, and I am practically free to decide"[103] Thus, as free agents, the clubs handed them the required transfer papers.

Deportivo Cali initially approached Guillermo Barbadillo from Sport Boys, a recognized international who participated in the 1947 South American Championship. Following the player's request, Sport Boy's board approved Barbadillo's move to Deportivo Cali in early May for the 1949 season.[104]

Humberto Salcedo Fernández, on behalf of América de Cali, was also seeking Peruvians. Unlike Deportivo Cali, they sought two of the sanctioned players: Valeriano López and Juan Lecca. Although neither of them went to América, the importance of Valeriano's figure is clear in El Relator's note as transcribed by the Peruvian La Crónica:

> We would like to inform our readers that Valeriano López is the best center forward that Peru currently has and the best new talent that Peruvian football has produced in recent years. We believe that with Valeriano's inclusion in the popular 'red' team ranks, it will become the most serious contender for this year's professional championship.[105]

In early May, the Peruvian press began reporting on the exodus. Guillermo Barbadillo moved to Cali. Others followed suit, such as Víctor Passalacqua (from Ciclista), Antonio García (Jorge Chávez Callao), Luis Salazar (Unión Callao), and, a couple of weeks later, Máximo "Vides" Mosquera (Sporting Tabaco).[106] It was not only Deportivo Cali that showed interest in Peruvian players. Alfredo Mosquera (Municipal) signed for Millonarios just a few weeks later. With no contract, the Mosquera brothers, Alfredo and "Vides", left the country with the paperwork in order.[107]

The players involved in the *Las Palmas* affair found a window to solve their situation. Barbadillo recommended Valeriano to Cali, but, given his situation in Peru, Rivera Gómez initially offered him a position as coach of the third-division squad.

Valeriano, known as the *Tanque de Casma* (Tank of Casma, his birthplace), was just 22 years old when he decided to accept Cali's offer to coach the academy team. Or so he claimed. Sport Boys, his club, was affected by his departure, and he claimed it would be a mockery if he found a job as a coach in the country or abroad. They argued that "players banished for life for violating sporting ethics travel to work as coaches when it is very easy to understand that a coach must have more sporting ethics than the player himself".[108] Thus, Sport Boys refused to deliver the transfer papers.

Valeriano wrote a letter to Leoncio Gómez, the President of the Football Federation, asking for permission to travel because, having been denied the opportunity to play football, "he was in a situation of barely being able to survive".[109] They restrained him from playing football, but also intended to ban him from working in the football industry. The response was negative, and Valeriano had to sue to fly to Colombia to work. On August 4, 1949, Valeriano López finally arrived in Cali, where his main job was not to train in the academy. He made his debut on August 14 against Atlético Bucaramanga, scoring two goals and providing two assists in a 6-1 victory.

Incidentally, all players involved in the *Las Palmas* affair played in Colombia during the *El Dorado* era. Valeriano López and Eliseo Morales joined Deportivo Cali, Juan Lecca played for Once Deportivo, and, at the dusk of *El*

*Dorado*, for Deportivo Cali. Felix Mina, Juan Castillo, and René Rosasco all signed with Independiente Medellín.

The story behind Peru's exodus to Colombia predated the Argentine migration and was facilitated by several factors: the amateur status of Peru's league, which resulted in low salaries; a surprisingly flexible labor market for that era, which allowed players to cross the border without Colombian teams paying transfer fees; and the draconian measures imposed after the *Las Palmas* affair.

### *Paraguay*

Between 1948 and 1954, an exodus of Paraguayan players occurred as players departed their homeland for professional leagues in Italy, Argentina, Uruguay, and Colombia. This migration stemmed from three interconnected factors: Paraguay's promising yet underdeveloped football infrastructure, the political and economic turmoil engulfing the nation in the late 1940s, and the lucrative opportunities presented by Colombian clubs. The convergence of these circumstances created conditions that drew many, if not most, of Paraguay's top-level players abroad, reshaping the domestic football landscape for years to come.

Paraguay, a nation scarred by historical conflicts and economic struggles, surprisingly cultivated a competitive football culture during the first half of the twentieth century. Despite the lingering aftereffects of the War of the Triple Alliance and subsequent economic crises, the nation nurtured a domestic championship renowned for its intensity. While influenced by its neighbors—Argentina, Brazil, and Uruguay—Paraguayan football developed a distinct identity. Its competitive spirit was evident in the national team's strong performance at the South American Championship.

Following patterns established in other regions, a central component of this footballing exodus was Paraguay's entrenched marronism system. As historian Miguel Ángel Bestard documented, Paraguayan football operated within an informal economy where players received inconsistent, arbitrary compensation without the protections of a regulated professional framework.[110] This institutional uncertainty created fertile ground for talented footballers to seek more reliable opportunities abroad, where formal contracts and consistent salaries offered financial security.[111]

Political upheaval shaped the period preceding this footballing exodus. In 1947, Paraguay descended into its most catastrophic internal conflict of the twentieth century—a civil war that ravaged the nation. The violent turmoil fractured Paraguayan society, creating profound economic and social instability. Indeed, the conflict's lasting social and economic repercussions accelerated the departure of sporting talent, transforming what might have been individual career decisions into a collective migration driven by necessity.[112] Deportivo Pereira and Cali's Boca Juniors emerged as primary destinations for Paraguayan talent. The Colombian league's financial incentives and promise of exposure drew many Paraguayans.

Among the players who migrated to Colombia, César López Fretes stands out. Already a prominent captain and key figure of the national team, López Fretes joined Deportivo Pereira in 1949. His leadership on and off the pitch proved instrumental. Much like the Argentine Pedernera—who had a similar effect on Millonarios—López Fretes served as a bridge, attracting more Paraguayan talent to the Colombian league. Other Paraguayan players who followed Fretes to Pereira included Carmelo Colombo, Enrique Ávalos, and Marcelino Vargas. Another Paraguayan standout was Atilio López, who joined Boca Juniors in 1950 and played for Atlético de Madrid for three seasons between 1953 and 1956.

Millonarios also had their Paraguayan star, Julio César Ramírez, who would be part of the illustrious eleven that made history, but who had an unfortunate debut on July 16, 1950, losing 0–1 against Universidad.

### *Uruguay*

The Uruguayan situation mirrored the Argentine situation, with players also going on strike, but with a different outcome. In 1949, the clubs had almost complete control over the footballers after they signed a contract. Whether to transfer a player or terminate his contract, the decision rested with the club, despite common delays in salary payments, lower than in Argentina.[113] Significantly, for what happened later, even when going abroad, upon returning, their transfer pass remained an asset of the original Uruguayan team.

The clubs refused to recognize the Uruguayan Union upon its foundation in August 1946. The players declared the strike in October 1948, which lasted until May 1949. The Uruguayan league was suspended, and no champion was ever declared.

The Union's achievements included securing 10% transfer fees for players when sold between clubs, establishing mandatory contract offers or freedom of action for players under 21, and abolishing the oppressive regulations and practices that had previously given clubs absolute control over players' careers. Free agency allowed players to move to Colombia without the club's consent.[114]

### *England*

The affair between English players and their clubs closely resembles what happened in Argentina. There was a salary cap, and the players had no free agency. When the Players' Union sought higher salaries, it declared a strike in 1946, which was declared illegal. Still, following the illegal strike, the National Arbitration Tribunal intervened and, in March 1946, ruled that the maximum wage would rise from £10 to £12 a week.[115] Compared with a factory worker, who earned between £4 and £5 a week, their compensation was more than competitive. They knew they were the main attraction in a show that drew thousands of spectators week after week.[116] Thus, many players were unhappy with the situation.

While several English players made the journey, no more than five played in Colombia. The man behind their arrival was Luis Robledo, a co-founder of Santa Fe. The 1948 champion of the first professional league saw how Millonarios and Deportivo Cali powered up with the best of Argentina and Peru, sending Santa Fe to third place in 1949.

Robledo's intentions coincided with Neil Franklin's frustrations, leading to an unexpected outcome. Franklin, a unionist in spirit and a Stoke player since he was a kid, was a formidable center-half who earned 27 caps between 1946 and 1950.[117] At the end of the 1948–1949 season, unhappy with Stoke's manager, for his criticism of his playing style and with the local press against him, he asked for a transfer request.

The club denied the transfer request in a very offensive manner. It is said that the directors kept him waiting for three hours while discussing the matter, after which, without receiving him, they denied the request.[118] Adding to the story, there were rumors that Stoke rejected a £30,000 (USD 84,000) offer from Hull City.

Franklin, unable to increase his income and a victim of the existing retain-and-transfer system, decided to force his exit at the start of the 1949–1950 season by refusing to sign the forms Stoke requested. He finally signed, but his frustration was such that he was planning a one-person strike by the end of that season. It was then, circa November 1949, that Robledo sent a letter addressed to Neil Franklin to Stoke City's offices.[119] Unaware of its contents, which offered enormous financial benefits, the club passed on the letter to the player.

Franklin replied to Robledo, who, in turn, explained that there was no need for Stoke City to approve the transfer. Franklin pulled his teammate George Mountford and arrived in Bogota on May 10, 1950. Coincidentally, as Santa Fe fans received Franklin and Mountford as movie stars in Bogota, Manchester United played its first-ever North American game in Toronto.

Under Matt Busby's direction, Manchester United played twelve games. The tour ended on June 20, 1950, with the club richer, but the players with "now't in the bank to show for".[120] In New York, ready to return to England, Robledo called Charlie Mitten, the left-winger whom Franklin had recommended as the best in the world. With a similar rogue spirit as Neil, by July 13, 1950, Mitten had already played his first game with Santa Fe.

Santa Fe and Millonarios poached other British players, with some rumors maybe unfounded. When dealing with Mitten, his teammates Harry Cockburn and Jonny Aston rejected Santa Fe's offer upon returning from Brazil's World Cup, as did John Grosman (Blackpool).[121] Millonarios, meanwhile, had a representative in England, Jock Dodds, who, working on commission, claimed to have 250 players willing to travel to South America.[122] His success was questionable, given that only Billy Higgins (Everton) and Bobby Flavell

(Hearts—Scotland) signed contracts with Millonarios, while others, such as Jack Hedley (Everton) and Roy Paul (Swansea), spent only a few days in Colombia.[123] Still, this came at a cost. Upon return, Everton did not want to retain Hedley, selling him to Swansea.[124]

The presence of top British players underscores the relevance of El Dorado as the first multinational football league. Crossing the Atlantic was an adventure on its own. Franklin, for instance, first flew from London to Ireland, jumping next to Newfoundland and Labrador in Canada. Flying with his pregnant wife, George Mountford, and their two daughters, the next stop was New York. They left the Big Apple for Miami, heading next to Cuba and then Jamaica. The final stage of the trip took them to Barranquilla and, finally, Bogota. Eight flights and seven countries.[125]

### *Other nationalities*

Colombia had players from many nationalities at the time, including Italians, Spaniards, Costa Ricans, Ecuadorians, and Brazilians, among others. On the latter, as discussed earlier, Junior was expelled from Dimayor in 1949. Having no reason to return, while they negotiated readmission, the team played friendlies across Brazil.

Mario Abello traveled with the team and started working on the 1950 roaster. Brazilians were a natural choice, and Abello had learned that to lure them into traveling, he had to make sure to let them know that Barranquilla was next to the beautiful Caribbean beaches: "without any beaches, they would not travel".[126]

Thus, early in 1950, Abello negotiated with several Brazilian players, Marcelo (Flamengo), Elba de Pádua Lima—Tim, and Heleno de Freitas (Vasco da Gama). At 35, Tim, a major star of the Brazilian team that finished third in the 1938 World Cup in France, was close to retirement. Heleno, on the other hand, was a superstar. A complex personality, he had played for Boca Juniors (Argentina) in 1948.

On March 7, 1950, Junior paid USD20,000 for Heleno de Freitas, Tim, Melinho Rodriguez de Oliveira (Botafogo), Sebastián Beracochea (Uruguayan, but playing for Botafogo), and Botafogo's starting goalkeeper, Ary Nogueira Cezar. The Brazilian teams protested, as the Argentines had done before, and the English clubs would soon do. Even so, Abello managed to fly to Barranquilla with the five players hired in Brazil on March 11, 1950.

Anecdotally, while Botafogo played in Venezuela a month later, Abello flew there and hired three additional players: Gerson Dos Santos, Octavio Sergio Morales, and Egidio Landolfi. The latter two were injured before flying to Barranquilla and thus returned to Brazil, never managing to play for Junior.[127]

With the end of World War II, Hungary became, by 1949, a Soviet satellite. Between 1949 and 1952, the communists executed 2,000 people and imprisoned 100,000 more.[128] Meanwhile, following Soviet doctrine, the government reorganized sports, bringing them under central direction. In football, the most significant move was transforming the Kispest Football Club into Honved, which, together with players from MTK, served as the foundation for the great Hungarian team of the first half of the 1950s.[129] Politics and sports compromised livelihood, enough reason for many to flee the country.

Lázlo Kubala, the most famous Hungarian exile, followed a similar path. He went to Italy hoping to play and start a new life. Hungary, however, as a FIFA member, demanded that these players be sanctioned for leaving their clubs without authorization. Although some managed to play, FIFA complied with others, including Kubala. Lázlo had no choice but to join Hungaria, a team of political refugees mainly from Hungary but also from other European countries.

In November 1950, Hungaria arrived in Colombia, prompting the Italian press to complain about the escape of "thirteen of the best Hungarian players currently playing in Italy". [130] Kubala, whose arrival was perpetually imminent, never came.

Absent Kubala, the team still had some stars in its squad. Among them, Gyula Zsengellér, who played with Hungary in the 1938 World Cup, was in the final against Italy and, with five goals, shared the second place in the tournament's Golden Boot trophy.

Hungaria played eight games in Colombia between November 1950 and January 1951, losing six and drawing just two. Still, Junior hired four players from that team: Imre Danko, Wladislaw Szoke, Bela Sarosi, and Bela Majtenyi. Deportivo Samarios, from Santa Marta, entrant in the 1951 league, hired several players from Hungaria, including Zsengellér, who played for two seasons, scoring 23 goals in 37 games. Another seven Hungarians stayed in Santa Marta, including Torok and Gyorgy Marik. Samarios further hired Negrescu (Romanian), Strittich (Austrian), Hanke (Czechoslovakia), and the Italian goalkeeper Di Lorenzo, who left shortly after signing the contract.[131]

The Austrians, Ernst Sabeditsch and Rudolf "Rudi" Strittich, had their lives changed when their team, First Vienna, returning from the Middle East, stopped in Beirut. Sabeditsch accepted 850 grams of raw opium, which he offered to share with Rudi and a third partner, Schaffer. Once in Vienna, Sabeditsch tried to sell the drugs in a café, but police informants spotted him. Rudi and Schaffer were sentenced to three months in prison, while Sabeditsch was sentenced to five. Despite being a minor offense, the Austrian Football Association (ÖFB) banned them for a year. Rudi moved to Triestina, where he served as youth coach under the future legend Bela Gutmann, but could not play for the team because ÖFB would not deliver the transfer papers. It was then that Rudi received a message from Sabeditsch asking him to join him on a team in Colombia—the signing bonus: USD 5,000.[132] It remains unclear who contacted Sabeditsch, who broke his ankle, during the first game. Rudi played for the 1951 season, with relative success, but returned home in November as he failed to reach an agreement with the club.[133]

Milos Dragolovic had to leave Yugoslavia for political reasons after the war. He moved to Peru in search of new opportunities and found work at a textile factory. After a couple of years, FIFA allowed him to play, and he performed successfully for the 1948 Sport Boys squad. A Cúcuta fan hired him and paid all expenses to bring him to Colombia.[134] He later played for Universidad in 1952.

## The golden days

The oral history of El Dorado tells that it had the best players in the world and that stadiums were constantly full of fans. The former is arguably true. If not all, it did bring together most of the best South American players of the time, along with more than a handful of European stars. The latter requires further explanation.

### *Salaries*

As noted, lacking a contract with any Argentine club and without transfer papers from Huracán, Pedernera flew to Bogota in June 1949. He was the first megastar to accept the challenge of playing in the Dimayor league.

The idea of bringing top stars was born before Pedernera's arrival. In May 1949, the Colombian press reported that "several teams" were considering inviting some of Argentina's biggest stars, including Pontoni, Martino, Di Stéfano, and Pedernera, to play in the league for a few months.[135] Aware of the strike, they saw an opportunity. The strike, however, ended, and there is no record of such invitations. Meanwhile, América, Cali, and Millonarios, taking advantage of the Peruvian situation, did bring players to their teams.

In May 1949, Deportivo Cali brought in Peruvian star Guillermo Barbadillo, along with Víctor Passalacqua, Antonio García, and Luis Salazar.[136] Later that month, the Mosquera brothers, major Peruvian stars, moved to Deportivo Cali (Máximo, "Vides") and Millonarios (Alfredo). For the latter, the star of the Peruvian national team during the 1949 South American Championship, sources suggest that he received a signing fee of USD 2,000, plus COP 500 (USD 255) per month.[137] Note that Alfredo Mosquera left his club, Tabaco, with the club's permission having expired his contract.[138]

Preparing for the 1949 season, Millonarios had hired the Argentine Carlos "Cacho" Aldabe, who officed as player and eventually as coach. Familiar with the situation in Argentina, Aldabe pressed Alfonso Senior to bring Pedernera to Bogota. Millonarios sent Aldabe to Argentina and received a telegram in late May stating that "*Adolfo Pedernera ready to travel to Colombia. Joining Millonarios with conditions. First-class passage for him and his wife. Five thousand dollar annual bonus and apartment rental*".[139]

The amount was out of proportion as the typical gate receipts for a given match day were around USD 5,000.[140] The discussions at the club's board meeting were intense, but eventually Senior agreed, and Pedernera arrived in

Colombia on June 10, 1949. "5,000 fans, 2,000 cars, and 25 buses" received the superstar at Bogota's airport.[141]

He went to the stadium on June 12 for the game between Millonarios and Atlético Municipal (later Atlético Nacional). The approximately 15,000 fans who attended the game were enough to fund the USD 5,000, with money to spare.[142] Senior, Millonarios, Dimayor, had found the recipe for success. The impact of Pedernera's arrival in Colombia was such that, in a public office, they had to put up a banner reading, "It is prohibited to talk about Pedernera during office hours".[143]

Perdernera's signing bonus of USD 5,000 clearly covers and exceeds the ARS 1,500 (USD 311) salary cap in Argentina. The monthly salary of COP 1,500 (USD 765) adds another USD 9,180 to his yearly income. Lastly, there was a winning bonus that varied by player (and the precise figure for Pedernera remains unknown), typically around COP 300 per match won and COP 150 per draw. These figures imply that Pedernera earned approximately USD 13,700 over the seven months he played after he arrived in 1949, translating to an annual income of approximately USD 23,500.

Much of the data on salaries is noisy and, for the most part, based on rumors. At the time, players flying from Argentina to Colombia typically had a layover in Lima (Peru). While resting, even spending a day, the Peruvian press would interview the football stars. The reporter asked Pedernera if it was true that he had signed for COP 100,000, just over USD 51,000. Simultaneously, he inquired if it was true that he did not have the transfer papers. Pedernera's answer was, "Well, the journalist is right when he says that he is everywhere, even in the eye of a needle".[144] Months later, Pedernera said that, still lacking a contract, given all the fuss related to his arrival, he claimed that he was short of cash and needed ARS 10,000 (approximately USD 2,000). The club officials took him to the treasury and, without any receipt, gave him the money.[145] Considering the payments to other stars who followed Pedernera to Colombia, it may be true that the amount was COP 100,000, perhaps over a two-year period. Whatever the figure, Millonarios paid Pedernera's talent very well.

By July 1949, Pedernera was recommending other players, and petitions were ultimately attended in both Colombia and Argentina. It was his credibility, given his status, that gave *El Dorado* the decisive push. He started humbly, initially recommending Oscar Corzo, a Huracán player who, like Pedernera, lacked a contract. Millonarios offered Corzo a signing bonus of ARS 30,000 (USD 6,240), a monthly salary of ARS 900 (USD 87), plus "usual bonuses", an offer impossible to reject.[146] While in Lima for his layover, Corzo confirmed these figures and explained that the bonuses were for games won, goal difference, and points earned. He also confirmed that he was traveling without the transfer papers from either Huracán or AFA.[147]

The financial success of Pedernera's signing encouraged other teams to pursue Argentine stars of their own. The players moved to Colombia following the money, of course, but also because they resented the way the clubs treated footballers. Such is the case of Manuel "Colorado" Giúdice, who, together with Luis Ferreyra, flew to Deportivo Cali in 1949. He argued that Platense had expelled him in retaliation and that only a teammate's injury had allowed him to play. At 31, ensuring his future was a priority. Thus, showing his contract to the reporter, the ARS 40,000 (USD 8,300) signing fee and ARS 1,800 (USD 374) monthly salary convinced him to play in Colombia.[148] Luis Ferreyra had the same offer as Giúdice.

While Giúdice and Ferreyra left Argentina, some, like Raúl Leguizamón, decided to stay, but for smaller figures. Leguizamón, for instance, signed for Atlanta (ARG) for a fee of ARS 15,000 (approximately USD 3,100) and a monthly salary of ARS 1,200 (approximately USD 250).[149] Giúdice played for Deportivo Cali until June 1951, when he received a note from the club notifying him that "effective as of this date, we have decided to remove the bonuses to which you were entitled".[150] He had been alternating between player and coach. At almost 33, he chose to retire and return to Buenos Aires.

Soon enough, Pedernera and Millonarios targeted the best players Argentina had to offer: River Plate stars Alfredo Di Stéfano, an exceptional young forward, and Néstor Raúl "Pipo" Rossi, center half. Rumors had it that Torino (Italy) was interested in offering River Plate up to ARS 220,000 (USD 45,700) for Rossi, an amount still far from the player's value, according to the Argentines.[151] Di Stéfano, unhappy with his income at River Plate, was also considering Torino, which offered up to ARS 600,000 (USD 125,000).[152] Colombia became a bargaining chip in Argentina. While negotiating with River Plate, Rossi, Di Stéfano, and Ferrari announced the Colombian offers.[153]

Pedernera had flown to Colombia alone, leaving his pregnant wife behind, because the due date was too close. After a 3-3 draw away to the powerful Deportivo Cali, and given a two-week recess in the league, he went to Argentina in early August 1949. Officially, he was checking on his wife, but he had another not-so-secret mission: to bring Di Stéfano and Rossi.[154]

On August 8, 1949, Di Stéfano told a reporter that he was not leaving Argentina because he had a meeting with River Plate officials the day after, when they would approve his requests. However, on August 2, just a couple of days after arriving, Pedernera had reserved plane tickets for Colombia on behalf of two anonymous individuals. Not until August 8, when he paid ARS 5,000 (USD 1,040) for the tickets, did he disclose the names: Alfredo Di Stéfano and Néstor Raúl Rossi. The next day, at the airport, Pedernera still stated that "he was not a football agent", denying his involvement in Di Stefano's and Rossi's move to Colombia.[155]

Unlike Pedernera, who left without a contract, Di Stéfano and Rossi, although under coercion, had signed with River Plate for the monthly sum of ARS 1,500 (USD 311) and ARS 150 (USD 31,1) per point earned.[156] While at the airport, both sent a message to River Plate terminating the contract due to the club's unpaid Christmas bonuses and other outstanding payments.[157] The legal argument was that, because the club was in debt, it could not enforce the contract. The River Plate magazine would call them "football stowaways".[158] In his memoirs, Di Stéfano—speaking in the plural, implying that Rossi received the same terms—recalls a USD 12,000 signing bonus, a monthly salary of COP 1,200 (USD 612), and COP 300 per win.[159] Including friendlies, Millonarios won 16 games with Di Stéfano, which implies that his 1949 income for half a year in Colombia was around USD 20,500. Rossi received a similar amount, but like others, his income stream increased with publicity. Shortly after his arrival, Rossi was receiving COP 100 (USD 51) daily to use the clothes of a particular establishment.[160]

The expectation for their debut was at the highest level. Six thousand fans went to the airport to receive Di Stéfano, Rossi, and Pedernera on August 11, 1949.[161] On a rainy pitch, the superstars' debut was on August 14 against Deportivo Barranquilla, the team that had replaced Junior, with Di Stéfano scoring the fifth and last goal. Changes were radical since the amateur days just a few years earlier. In 1946, the Millonarios' monthly payroll was COP 1,500 (USD 800). The figure at the end of 1951, in a team full of stars, was COP 27,000 (USD 13,800).[162]

That same day, in Cali, Valeriano López, the Peruvian superstar, also made his debut, giving birth to Deportivo Cali's *rodillo negro*, the "black steamroller", together with fellow Peruvians Guillermo Barbadillo and Máximo Mosquera. Playing against Bucaramanga, Deportivo Cali won 6-1, with Valeriano and Barbadillo scoring two goals each, and Mosquera adding one (despite also missing a penalty kick). Valeriano López had agreed to move for a signing bonus of S/. 25,000 (USD $1,670), and a monthly salary of S/. 4,000 (USD 267).[163] Not common at the time, the Peruvian opened a bank account, checkbook included, but, bohemian as he was, a month later, he had no funds in the bank.[164]

Argentines and Peruvians flocked in masse to Colombia. Following Deportivo Cali's steps, Medellín brought in Peruvians, expecting to field a team of "ten Peruvian and one Argentine" against Huracán in a match played on August 28, 1949.[165] Peruvians had been arriving in Medellin over the past three weeks. On August 11, Enrique Perales arrived in Medellin from Mexico. From Lima, Reinaldo Luna arrived, having been released by his club, which had decided not to renew his contract.

Additionally, Felix Mina, who had been banned for life in Peru after the *Las Palmas* affaire, arrived in Medellin.[166] Eventually, Medellín, particularly the 1950 squad, became known as *La Danza del Sol*, the Dance of the Sun, because they played "fascinating like an Incan ritual dance, glorious like the dance of the sun".[167]

There were still plenty of superstars in Argentina willing to come. Rene Pontoni, above all. South American champion with Argentina in 1945, 1946, and 1947, he was the starter in the latter, even as the young Alfredo Di Stéfano pushed for a place in the starting eleven. Di Stéfano scored six goals during the tournament, taking advantage of Pontoni's muscle strain in the second game against Bolivia. He made his comeback, playing 25 minutes in the second-to-last fixture and starting in the decisive 3-1 win against Uruguay on December 28.[168] While Pedernera, Di Stéfano, and Rossi were moving to Colombia, Pontoni was again injured. Operated in the last week of June 1949, he returned to the pitch but would never be the same.

Santa Fe won the first professional league in 1948. Pontoni was a reasonable catch, but before him, Santa Fe went for Ángel Perucca, *el portón de América*, the "Gate of America", who was a center-half at the level of Rossi. Before his departure, he wrote an open letter explaining his move.[169] Like others, he complained that he was forced to sign his contract, but he had explicitly informed his club, San Lorenzo, that for ARS 1,500 (USD 311) a month, he would not play. He stated that he asked San Lorenzo for a loan of ARS 10,000 (USD 2,080) for a business initiative, under the understanding that it was an advance on future payments. However, over time, he only received ARS 1,500 plus standard bonuses. Then, Santa Fe approached him. A reporter seeks to confirm that the Colombian offer was for ARS 250,000 (USD 51,975) for two years, ARS 3,200 (USD 665) monthly salary, ARS 400 (USD 83) for a game won, and COP 350 (USD 180) each month for a technical assistant to the team. His response, confirming the amounts, was, "I was speechless with that offer".[170] In this case, since the offers were made in September and the source is dated to the same month, we use the exchange rate before the devaluation. However, one tends to believe that the figures are too high and would make more sense with October's exchange rate: ARS 250,000 (USD 27,700). In any case, at 30, it was a lifetime opportunity. These figures put into perspective the ARS 100,000 paid to Pedernera, according to the Peruvian reporter. The ARS 10,000 that San Lorenzo lent Perucca, he made it clear that he returned the money.

Perucca flew to Colombia in October, together with Mario Fernández and Adolfo Benegas. Fernández's offer was ARS 180,000 (USD 37,422), having received ARS 50,000 (USD 10,400) in Argentina before boarding the plane.[171] Pontoni, three months after his knee surgery, in early October 1949, accepted Santa Fe's offer which in his own words amounted to ARS 250,000 (USD 27,700) for two years, ARS 3,200 (USD 354) monthly salary, ARS 400 (USD 44) for a game won, and COP 300 (USD 153) each month for a technical assistant to the team.[172] In anticipation of the expectations raised, Santa Fe chartered a "great number of buses from San Diego Park to *Techo* airport" to greet the star. Thousands showed up.

On October 25, Pontoni flew with Santa Fe to Medellin to play Atlético Municipal. Against the doctor's orders, he decided to play for no more than 20 minutes. Unlucky for him, his injured knee did not resist the charge of a rival. Pontoni returned to Argentina to see his doctor, while Santa Fe not only honored his contract but also offered him a two-month leave and plane tickets for his wife and daughter.[173]

Colombia's interest in Argentine players continued in 1950, allowing many to use it as a bargaining chip while negotiating with local clubs. Felix Loustau, a member of *La Maquina*, "the Machine", together with Juan Carlos Muñoz, José Manuel Moreno, Adolfo Pedernera, and Ángel Labruna, formed the formidable forward lineup of the 1940s River Plate. According to Loustau, at some point in late 1949, Carlos Sarmiento Lora, wanting to take him to Deportivo Cali, offered him USD18,000 for two years.[174] Loustau gave River Plate a 23-hour deadline, and when he learned that River Plate had not considered his case, he signed with Cali, received an advance payment of USD 8,000, and committed to flying in February after undergoing appendicitis surgery.

Antonio Liberti, president of River Plate, bumped into Loustau on the street and took him to the club's offices. He gave him ARS 180,000 (USD 20,000) for two years and ARS 4,000 (USD 440) per month. Where did the salary cap go? Indeed, he was the first to openly receive such a large amount, encouraging other players to demand payments over the cap.[175]

Loustau claims that when he went to return the money to Lora, he rejected an additional USD 5,000, but had to offer River Plate two houses (his and his father's) as collateral for the contract they offered him. The latter was a safeguard against possible additional offers for the player. Deportivo Cali, now with the Argentine Carlos Peucelle as a coach, did not leave empty-handed. Vilariño, from Rosario Central, was the player that Cali hired instead of Loustau. They also hired Castro, whom Independiente had suspended and fined. Both traveled to Colombia, lured by an offer of ARS 180,000 (USD 20,000) for a two-year contract and, at least in Vilariño's case, a monthly salary of ARS 5,000 (USD 550).[176] Vilariño left because Rosario Central, unwilling to sell him, would not accept his demands. With negotiations open, Cali officials knew Vilariño could still receive a significant offer from Central. Thus, to avoid losing the player, as they had lost Loustau, on the scheduled day to fly to Colombia, they left the hotel in Buenos Aires very early in the morning with Vilariño and remained hidden until they reappeared at the airport. The player's complaints about the situation only got him to fly under the promise that he would return if Central transferred him to another club.

Months earlier, in August 1949, the Universidad de Bogota had brought in Osvaldo Pérez from Rosario Central. Boca Juniors (ARG) offered ARS 200,000 (USD 41,000) for the transfer, but Central, due to governance issues, made no decision.[177] Thus, Pérez flew, and, according to the Colombian press, received COP 50,000 (USD 25,500)—presumably for two years—and COP 2,500 (USD 1,275) per month.[178] In a later interview, he mentions that his offer was USD 8,400, that he received USD 5,100 upon arrival, and that he was promised the rest by the end of the year.[179]

Pérez made history in 1950 as the first player traded within the Colombian league. Deportivo Cali paid Universidad COP 20,000 (USD 10,200) plus ARS 80,000 (USD 8,800) for the player, including the USD 3,100 that

Universitario still owed him.[180] He was also the first big name to attempt a return to Argentina. In January 1950, while on Christmas holidays, he gave an interview expressing his satisfaction with being able to play for Boca Juniors, who, according to him, had paid Central ARS 30,000 (USD 3,325) plus two friendlies with ARS 50,000 (USD 5,540) per game guaranteed for Central.[181] He wanted to return because he had been unable to integrate with his compatriots in Colombia, who would rough him up during matches, remembering that he had been one of the first to side with the clubs during the strike and play contrary to the FAA's position. He miscalculated. He told AFA that, despite his trip to Colombia, he had not played, but soon the AFA disciplinary tribunal received reports that he had played at least 11 matches. Even Boca Juniors and Rosario Central voted to remove Pérez from the player registry. He had no choice but to return to Colombia.

Liberti, River's President, tried to convince Rossi and Di Stéfano to stay in Argentina following the Christmas holidays. Di Stéfano, who had taken advantage of the December holiday trip to get married and whose wife wanted to stay in Buenos Aires, received an offer of ARS 300,000 (USD 33,200) plus ARS 150 (USD 16,6) per point earned. Di Stéfano replied that River would also have to reimburse Millonarios, noting that, up to August 1949, he had received ARS 180,000 (USD 20,000 using January's 1950 exchange rate, or around USD 37,400 using August's 1949 exchange rate).[182] Of course, Di Stéfano and all other players were expelled from AFA, and although they hoped to return for the proper amount of money, the amnesty would not come for years.

By 1950, many superstars were still in Argentina, including Julio Cozzi and Héctor "Pibe" Rial. Cozzi, the goalkeeper of Platense, wanted to move to Boca Juniors, which offered up to ARS 400,000 (USD 44,000). Platense, unwilling to accept any offer from an Argentine club, instead called Cozzi to sign a contract and pay him a monthly salary of ARS 3,000 (USD 330). His response was to sign for Millonarios, who were patiently waiting, for ARS 150,000 (USD 16,600) and a monthly salary of ARS 4,750 (USD 526), despite Platense eventually offering him ARS 120,000 (USD 13,300), composed of ARS 80,000 as a signing bonus, ARS 3,000 monthly salary, and ARS 150 per point earned.[183] Insufficient, Cozzi left for Millonarios, who were assembling what, for some, would be the best team in the world for the next two years. Cozzi's debut, however, was unfortunate. With hardly any training, Millonarios drew 3-3 against Boca Juniors in Bogota.

Héctor "el Pibe" Rial, "the kid" in Argentine slang, like Di Stéfano, traveled to Colombia at a very young age. While *la Saeta Rubia* arrived at 23, Rial arrived in April 1950 at 21. They were rivals in Colombia, but years later, they would play together in Real Madrid thanks to Di Stéfano's recommendation. Rial's signing bonus with Santa Fe was ARS 200,000 (USD 22,170), COP 1,000 (USD 510) per month, and COP 300 (USD 153) per game won.

The most extravagant collective signing of El Dorado was pulled off in 1951 by newcomers Quindío of Armenia. For their league debut, the club issued shares to the public to raise COP 75,000 (USD 38,265) needed to renovate San José Stadium and bring it up to first-division standards.[184] Quindío's story is tied to the dreams of José Próspero Fabrini and Emilio Moisés Reubens. Fabrini, a brief manager of Newell's Old Boys (ARG) in 1950, had playing experience at Newell's (ARG), where he made his debut, and at San Lorenzo (ARG). He was a man of the world, having played in Brazil (Esporte Clube Bahia), Chile (Audax Italiano), and at Nacional of Montevideo. Emilio Reuben, born in Canada, began his football career at Vélez Sarsfield (ARG) before going on to succeed at Independiente (ARG). With experience in Brazil, Chile, and Uruguay, Reuben arrived at Deportivo Cali in 1947 and played for the club during the inaugural 1948 season. In late 1950, at some café in Rosario (ARG), Fabrini and Reuben hatched the idea of assembling a group of players from the Santa Fe Province's second division to take to Colombia. The plan was to play exhibition matches and place the players in Colombia's booming football scene. Initially composed of 14 players, the Rosario group applied for passports to Peru in Argentina, then set their definitive course for Colombia. On January 15, 1951, brought in by Marco Fidel Varela, general manager of América de Cali, the newly formed Wander's made their debut against América, losing 5–4. The Argentine lineup was: Bianchi, Mandarino, Lombardo, Sánchez, Gonzalo, Carugno, Belén, Fabrini, Walton, Garelli, Urruti. In their first league match—Quindío's professional tournament debut—against Universitario in Bogota, the lineup read: Bianchi, Mandarino, Lombardo, Sánchez, Gonzalo, Carugno, Belén, Garelli, La Spina, Gómez, Urruti. All of them, except for Norberto Gómez, who came from Deportes Caldas, had arrived in Colombia with Wander's. Quindío, having been accepted into the 1951 professional tournament, promised both a stadium and a team. It solved the former in just two months thanks to the public share issue. The latter came even faster. On February 1, 1951, Nepomuceno Jaramillo, a businessman from the city of Armenia, signed a USD 35,000 bonus to hire the entire Wander's squad to represent Deportes Quindío. In addition to the signing bonus, the players shared a combined monthly salary of COP 12,000 (USD 4,781).[185]

The 1949 season concluded with no professional team in Barranquilla, as Deportivo Barranquilla withdrew from the competition in September due to financial difficulties. The impasse was resolved for the 1950 season when two city clubs joined Dimayor: Junior and Sporting.

Junior took advantage of its Brazilian experience and imported several top Brazilian players, above all, Heleno de Freitas. A star in Botofogo, where he had scored 209 goals in 235 games, was transferred to Boca Juniors in Argentina in 1948 for ARS 120,000 (USD 25,000).[186] Unhappy in Argentina, he decided to return to Brazil—Vasco da Gama—where he was considered the "best center-forward in Brazilian football".[187]

Mario Abello, Junior's general manager, went to Rio de Janeiro to bring reinforcements to Barranquilla, but faced strong opposition from Brazilian clubs. Still, offering Heleno USD 10,000 as a signing bonus for a two-year contract and a monthly salary of COP 1,000 (USD 510), he convinced the superstar to move to Barranquilla. Later reports, however, suggest that Heleno's monthly salary reached COP 2,000 (USD 1,020), the highest in the country.[188] However, on March 8, in Rio, Abella was detained by the police, accused by Botafogo of "illegal activities in trying to hire Brazilian football players".[189] Detained for 4 hours, he was released by 6 p.m., but was required to pay bail and to appear at the police station the following day. The authorities were accusing him of breaking the Brazilian penal code, which banned poaching workers. Fortunately for Abello, he managed to argue that such a rule made no sense when applied to artists and athletes. Overall, Abello's trip to Brazil was a success. In the same plane that brought Julio Cozzi to Colombia, Heleno flew from Rio to Barranquilla on March 9. He landed together with Elba de Padua Lima, *Tim*, Merinho Rodríguez de Olivero, Sebastián Beracochea (a Uruguayan player at Botafogo), and Botafogo's goalkeeper, Ary Nogueira Cezar.

With the highest expectations, Heleno's debut took place in Barranquilla, with over 9,000 fans generating revenue of COP 25,000 (USD 12,000) in a disappointing 0-0 draw against Bucaramanga. Contrary to Heleno's performance, Ary and Merinho's was praised by the press.[190] It would take time for Heleno to prove his worth. A week later, Boca Juniors beat Junior 5-0, a match in which the Caribbean side also fielded Romanian Negrescu. That night, Heleno threatened to return to Brazil after a fight in the hotel with teammate Rigoberto "me muerde" García, who blamed him for the defeat.[191]

With the Argentine and Peruvian markets saturated by 1949, other clubs began exploring alternatives.[192] Paraguay and Uruguay were natural choices. Pereira brought Carmelo Enrique Colombo in September 1949, the spearhead to bring more Paraguayan players. Then came Casimiro Ávalos. He played for Los Andes, a lower-division team in Argentina, on loan to Lanus in 1948, and then returned to Los Andes. Suggested by Carmelo, a high official in Pereira, Gabriel Cardona Rojas asked the Colombian consul in Buenos Aires to attend a performance by Ávalos. "After 20 days or a month had passed, Don Fabio replied to us, saying that that player was worth it because even though he didn't have much class, he was very fast and effective".[193] In 1950, in a tournament with stars such as Di Stéfano, Valeriano López, and Heleno, it was the Paraguayan Ávalos who finished as the league's top goalscorer with 27 goals and would be part of the Pereira team that finished third, behind Millonarios and Boca Juniors, in 1952.

There is no information on Ávalos' salary. There are reports that Avalo himself recalls a prominent doctor from Pereira, Carlos Ángel, offering him COP 100 (USD 51) for each goal scored during the 1950 season. By the end of the season, Ángel was worried about the money: he had to pay Ávalos

COP 3,900 (USD 1,990).[194] Following the 1950 World Cup in Brazil, Pereira brought in five more Paraguayans: Marcelino Vargas, Armando Gonzáles, Enrique Ávalos, César López Fretes, and Sixto Cantero.

Pereira was not the only team focused on Paraguayan players. Sporting (Barranquilla) and Boca Juniors (Cali) also had a significant number of players from that nationality. In February 1950, Sixto Noceda, Estanislao Romero, and Felix Lezcano arrived for the Caribbean team. The former two were part of the Paraguayan team that finished second in the 1949 South American Championship and were already selected for the 1950 World Cup. Interestingly, Barranquilla contemporary press reports that the players arrived with proper transfer papers from the Paraguayan League and their respective clubs: Presidente Hayes (PAR) in Noceda's case and River Plate (PAR) in the other two cases. The report suggests that the Paraguayan League respected the Sporting deal because it was formalized before the squad was announced for the World Cup. Beyond the apparent contradiction, the claim lacks credibility, mainly because in January 1950, the Paraguayan *Consejo Nacional de Deporte* banned player transfers to foreign clubs, amid concerns about the Colombian situation and the upcoming World Cup.[195] Yet it nonetheless reflects a widespread awareness in Colombia about the illicit nature of player imports.[196]

Throughout the entire 1950 season, Boca Juniors brought in players from Paraguay. In February, four players arrived: José Ocampos, Santiago Rivas, Alejandrino Genes, and Jerónimo Pereira. In March, Carlos Arce (Luqueño) and Marcial Barrios arrived from Venezuela. In that same batch was the Argentine Miguel Ortega, who claimed he had played in Italy; however, we found no record of that.[197] He arrived in Boca to serve as coach.

In November, Arce flew to Paraguay, returning with reinforcements: the goalkeeper Pablo Centurión (Cerro Porteño), Alberto Gonzales, Manuel Gavilán, Atilio López (Guaraní), José Luis Cañete, and Ángel Berni. Centurión and López were former members of the Paraguayan squad that successfully participated in the 1949 South American Championship. Although both Centurión and López also traveled to the World Cup, only López played, scoring the equalizer in the 2-2 draw against Sweden.

Atilio López and Berní would later be part of the Paraguayan squad that returned as champions from the 1953 South American Championship. The latter later moved to San Lorenzo and, in 1959, to Betis (Spain), where he played until 1963. The significance of Berni's and Lopez's story lies in the fact that they managed to play for the national team shortly after returning to Paraguay. The Paraguayan gamble paid for Boca Juniors. They finished fifth in 1950, but were runners-up in 1951 and 1952, only beaten by Millonarios. In 1953, Boca finished third.

Millonarios' Paraguayan Julio César Ramírez, a centerpiece of the machine that would become the Bogota club, arrived from Huracán in July 1950. He asked Huracán for permission to fly from Buenos Aires to Asunción to visit his family. He did see them, but he was really organizing his trip to Bogota after accepting a signing bonus of ARS 150,000 (16,630) plus a COP 1,000 (USD 510) monthly salary.[198]

In July 1950, Uruguay defeated Brazil in a packed Maracanã Stadium, with over 200,000 fans in attendance. The *Maracanazo* is, arguably, the most striking and unexpected result in the history of the World Cup. In the starting 11, the team included defender Eusebio Tejera and midfielder Schubert Gambetta, stars and World Cup Champions who joined Cúcuta Deportivo for the 1951 season.

They were not the first Uruguayans to arrive. Cúcuta sought for opportunities beyond Argentina and Peru, in their case, Uruguay. Their first hires occurred in February 1950 with Juan José Tulic, Juan Delucca, Julio Terra, Luis Alberto Luz, and Ramón Alberto Villaverde. The latter would move in 1952 to Millonarios and, later, in the summer of 1954, to FC Barcelona, where he played 162 games between 1954 and 1963.

Tejera and Gambetta arrived following a scouting trip from Cúcuta's vice-president, Pedro Nel Canal Ramírez, who also brought Juan Carlos Taibo (Champion with Nacional in the 1950 season), Bibiano Zapirain (Nacional), and Antonio Sacco (Rampla Juniors), who the contemporary press places as a former Racing Paris player. It turns out he did attempt to play in France, with little success, not with Racing but with the Red Star.[199] Zapirain, on the other hand, played for Inter Milan for two seasons, between 1946 and 1948, scoring 18 goals in 58 games.[200]

Uruguayan players also came lured by the money offered in Colombia. Gambetta points out that he was paid nothing for winning the World Cup and in Nacional (Uruguay) earned "almost nothing. Where I made some money was in Colombia, and I was able to buy my house".[201] There are few records of the salaries that Cúcuta paid to convince the Uruguayan stars. Some reports state that Tejera and Gambetta came for USD 4,000, while Sacco, Taibo, and Zapirain each came for USD 3,000.[202] The figures make sense given what we know other players were receiving at the time. Far from Millonarios, Cúcuta competed fiercely with the two Cali powerhouses to be the 1951 runners-up. By the end of the season, Cúcuta finished third, just one point behind Boca, and with the same number of points as Deportivo Cali. Cúcuta, however, was one of the two teams that managed to defeat *El Ballet Azul,* the only one away from Bogota.

Not only did South American players join *El Dorado*. Rumors in the contemporary press about negotiations with foreign stars were constant. In practice, for different reasons, only British and Hungarian players made the trip across the Atlantic in significant numbers. As mentioned, five British players arrived in Colombia in 1950: Neil Franklin, Charlie Mitten, George Mountford (Santa Fe), and Billy Higgins and Bobby Flavell (Millonarios).

Two additional players, Jack Hedley (not Jack Hardley nor Headley as written in the Colombian contemporary press and other accounts of *El Dorado*) and Roy Paul, arrived in June but returned to England within a week.[203] They refused to accept what they claimed were reduced terms relative to what they had been told before the trip.

Money, of course, was the driver for the British players. The information about the signing fee they received is noisy. When Charly Mitten talked with Robledo for the first time, he stated that Santa Fe is offering, for the "best left-winger in the world", the same offer as the others.[204] At the time, Robledo meant Franklin and Mountford, but if we assume that all British players received very similar offers, combining all sources might allow us to determine how much was enough to make them abandon home even under the threat of being vanished from English football.

Regarding Franklin's signing fee, estimates range from £1,500 (USD 4,200) to £10,000 (USD 28,000).[205] Others sources mention that he received a telegram stating, "Would you be interested to play for a South American club at a salary of £2,500 (USD 7,000) plus expenses".[206] Additional reports state that Franklin and Mountford left to earn USD 3,500 per annum.[207] The Colombian press reported in June 1950 that Millonarios (not Santa Fe) was trying to bring in Mitten, and that "Jonny Grosland"—probably meaning John Crosland (Blackpool)—had rejected a £4,000 (USD 11,200) offer from Santa Fe.[208]

Maybe Crosland realized that the offer was for a two-year contract. It seems there was confusion, possibly induced by how the offers were made, about the players' contract duration. Higgins, for instance, complains that the contract with Millonarios was for "two years, not twelve months", which would explain the disappointment of many of the UK players.[209]

Mitten speaks of "a £5,000 (USD 14,000) contract" signed by Franklin and Mountford, and told Matt Busby, United's coach, who had recently signed a £3,250 year contract, that he would make £5,000 as a signing fee, and an additional £5,000 as a yearly salary.[210] Overall, an educated guess of £5,000 for two-year contracts sounds reasonable.

To the signing fee, one must add the monthly salary. Mitten mentions a £5,000 (USD 14,000) yearly salary, which implies a monthly payment of COP 2,275. Given the figures reported for other stars, this seems unlikely. Moreover, the official immigration papers for Charlie Mitten report a monthly income of COP 1,000 (USD 510).[211] Reports mention a plausible monthly salary of £150 (USD 450) for Franklin.[212] However, press reports months later suggest that Mountford and Mitten earned COP 1,500 (USD 765), which, given the income of other stars, makes sense.[213] The winning bonus fluctuates between £7 (USD 20) for a win and £5 (USD 14) for a draw, as Franklin suggests, and the £35 (USD 98) per win that Mitten claims Franklin, Mountford, and himself received. The latter seems more plausible.

Thus, with a signing fee of USD 7,000 per year, a monthly salary of USD 765, and a winning bonus of USD 98, based on Santa Fe's 1950 winning game count, the typical annual income for a British player would be around USD 18,500.

Whatever the figure, it was way above what Franklin made in England. His total income during the 1948–1949 season was approximately £1,197 (USD 3,350). This figure includes all his earnings, including when playing for England.[214] In Colombia, they would make more than five times what they made in England.

Franklin lasted only a couple of months, unhappy with almost every aspect of life in Colombia, including the Argentines' hostility toward British players. Not surprisingly, he left on July 6, 1950, just days after England's disastrous World Cup campaign, where the national team—playing without Franklin—was eliminated after shocking defeats to Spain and the United States. In October 1950, Higgins left, and Flavell in December.

According to the legendary Stanley Matthews, Franklin only made £60 (USD 168) during his eight-week journey in Colombia, a figure that is not credible given that Colombian clubs used to pay at least half, in advance or upon signing the contract.[215] Charlie Mitten, by contrast, was successful in Santa Fe, and despite some complaints, he enjoyed life in Bogota. He mentions that the stadium's amenities were far ahead of those of the English League, that he played golf at the Country Club with Mountford, and that, unlike Franklin, the "sun always" shines.[216] Still, despite Santa Fe's offer to renew the contract, Mitten left on June 22, 1951. He was the last British player to return home.

Players from many other nationalities joined the league during its prime, from 1949 to 1951. As mentioned earlier, Hungaria arrived in November 1950, and despite their poor performance, many stayed in Colombia. They mostly played in Barranquilla with Junior and in Santa Marta with Deportivo Samarios. Most of them, however, did not last long. In June 1951, Samarios fired several players for poor performance, including the Argentine Rómulo Barrios, and the Hungarians Gerö Hindulaik and Kaljm. In Junior, for the 1952 season, only Majtenyi remained, leaving the club and the country in 1953. Hungarians were not the only Central Europeans to play in the Caribbean. Austrians and Czechs also played in Samarios. The Austrians Sabeditsch and Strittich, banned in Europe, had no problem—and probably no option—accepting the USD 5,000 signing fee to play in Santa Marta.

Pereira hired the Italian Luigi de Franco in August 1949, while he was working in Rosario (Argentina), to coach the team between 1949 and 1951. At the time, the Italian goalkeeper Angelo Bellotto was also in Argentina trying to play in their football league. Claims that he did not make it because he lacked the transfer papers made him an easy target for the Colombian league.[217] Before moving to Argentina, for reasons probably lost in time, he played for Arsenal Taranto in Serie B. He then tried new horizons, landing in Pereira by November 1949, where his performance was generally well-received.

At the start of the 1950 season, Pereira had one Italian, two Uruguayans, three Paraguayans, and four Colombians.[218] The club also had one Dominican

Republic player: the midfielder John López, who arrived before the professional era, in 1945, and was also a boxer.[219]

Universidad's boss, Daniel Hoyos Robledo, flew to Central America and opted for Costa Rican players for the 1950 season.[220] Initially arriving with seven players, whose debut resulted in a 2-0 loss against Millonarios in early April, others soon joined, including José Rafael "Fello" Meza, "Osito" Lozano, and Elías Valenciano. "Fello" Meza had played years earlier for Estudiantes de la Plata (Argentina) and then moved to Mexico, where Hoyos found him. Similarly, Valenciano had already played in the Mexican League.[221] Up to 21 Costa Rican Players eventually joined *El Dorado,* including Mario Murillo, who had also played in Mexico (Veracruz), and Evelio Alpizar, just 18 when he arrived. Information on the salaries of Costa Rican players is scarce, but some reports mention that "Fello" received a signing bonus of USD 3,000 and Valenciano received USD 6,000.[222]

Universidad also had Spaniards on its team: one in 1948 and the other in 1951. César Marriaga arrived first and only played for a season. Vicente Lapatza, a goalkeeper whom the Colombian contemporary press reports played for Baracaldo FC, came to Universidad from Erandia, a Basque team that played in the Spanish second division during the 1949–1950 season.[223] Upon relegation, it is unclear under what circumstances he moved to Colombia. He later moved to Junior but, upon its bankruptcy, traveled to Cuba with Deportivo Cali, where, in July 1953, they played against the First Division club Sporting de Gijón (Spain) and Centro Gallego (Cuba). The Asturian club picked him up and took him back to Spain.

A few Ecuadorians also came. In October 1947, during the Amateur era, the center half Enrique "Moscovita" Álvarez—international with his country and formerly with Lanus (Argentina)—played in Santa Fe. He left for the 1948 season, but returned to Santa Fe in February 1949. In 1950, he played for Emelec (Ecuador), but Neil Franklin must have seen him training before he left, because he describes him as "skinny, but technical midfield ball player".[224] Jorge Eduardo "Chompi" Henriquez moved from Audax Italiano (Chile) to Santa Fe in April 1949, then to Sporting de Barranquilla in 1950, where he played until 1952. Carlos Alume arrived at Once Deportivo in 1948. Twenty-one goals later, he left by the end of 1951. No information is available on the Ecuadorians' earnings.

Overall, it is challenging to determine the exact number of foreign players during El Dorado. Starting from a base of around 210 Colombians and 42 foreigners in 1948, press reports indicate 372 Colombians and 113 foreigners in 1949. Given 14 teams, the average roster size was 34 players.[225] The figure of Colombian players seems large, though the number of foreigners is more plausible: just over eight per team.

Additional reports show the number of players per club and nationality for the 1950 season (Table 2.1), indicating a total of 181 foreigners, just over 12 per club. Too many, too expensive.

*Table 2.1* Club and nationality of foreign players in the 1950 Colombian football season

| | *Argentina* | *Brazil* | *Chile* | *Costa Rica* | *Dominican Republic* | *Ecuador* | *English* | *Italy* | *Lithuania* | *Paraguay* | *Peruvian* | *Rumania* | *Uruguay* | *Total per Club* |
|---|---|---|---|---|---|---|---|---|---|---|---|---|---|---|
| America | 4 | | | | | | | | | | 9 | | | 13 |
| Atletico Bucaramanga | 6 | | | 2 | | | | | | | 2 | | | 10 |
| Atletico junior | | 8 | | | | | | | | | | 1 | | 9 |
| Boca juniors | | | | | | | | | | 8 | | | | 8 |
| Cucuta deportivo | 2 | | | | | | | | | | | | 10 | 12 |
| Deportes Caldas | 11 | | 2 | | | | | | 1 | | 1 | | | 15 |
| Deportivo Cali | 10 | | | | | | | | | | 5 | | | 15 |
| Deportivo Pereira | 2 | | | | 1 | | | 1 | | 5 | | | 2 | 11 |
| Huracán | | | | 2 | | | | | | | 5 | | 2 | 9 |
| Medellin | | | | 1 | | | | | | | 12 | | | 13 |
| Millonarios | 9 | 1 | | | | | 2 | | | | 2 | | 4 | 18 |
| Once deportivo | 8 | | | | | 1 | | | | | 4 | | | 13 |
| Santa Fe | 10 | | | | | | 3 | | | | | | | 13 |
| Sporting | 6 | | | | | 1 | | | | 5 | | | | 12 |
| Universidad | 1 | | | 9 | | | | | | | | | | 10 |
| Total nationality | 69 | 9 | 2 | 14 | 1 | 2 | 5 | 1 | 1 | 18 | 40 | 1 | 18 | 181 |

*Source:* El Heraldo, December 30, 1950, p. 9. and adding two English players for Millonarios.

### *Football in El Dorado*

Pedernera's debut was against Deportes Caldas on June 26, with the stadium El Campín at full capacity, 30,000 fans. He scored his first goal a week later against América in Cali in a 4–5 victory in the "best game ever witnessed over its entire sporting history".[226] He remained with Millonarios until 1954, though his appearances grew increasingly sporadic; by 1952, he featured in only a single official match. Over that period, he also served as the team's coach, with Rossi taking his place when Pedernera was absent.

Pedernera won six league titles with River Plate in Argentina and four with Millonarios in Colombia. He arrived at 30, left behind a unique legacy in Colombian football, and departed recognized by fans, pundits, and peers alike as one of the game's greatest players.

Pedernera was the pillar on which El Dorado was built. But it is Di Stéfano who gives the Colombian league the historical weight it has in football history. If Pedernera arrived at the end of his successful career, Di Stéfano developed the foundation of his legend in Colombia. The contemporary press acknowledges his extraordinary ability and his movement across the entire pitch—atypical for the era. But perhaps because, at some point, Di Stéfano chose not to give interviews, the same press praised other footballers just as highly: Valeriano López, Julio Cozzi, "el Pibe" Rial, and Néstor Raúl Rossi, among others. Yet his historical impact is quite different. Without question, thanks to his subsequent time at Real Madrid, Di Stéfano sits at the same table as Pelé, Cruyff, Maradona, and Messi. Di Stéfano arrived having just turned 23. It was during the El Dorado era that he completed his formation and established himself as the historically major star that he remains today. Much of the legend of El Dorado rests on his shoulders.

The Colombian people who lived in El Dorado gave birth to the legend, remembering the stars, the magic, the goals, the saves, and, of course, the imagery of full stadiums everywhere. Attendance is, hence, a central indicator to validate the truth behind the legend. Furthermore, the revenue that fans generate by attending stadiums helps explain the clubs' ability to assemble such a constellation of stars.

To track attendance between 1948 and 1953, we collected a unique dataset comprising 1,843 official (66,1%) and friendly (33,9%) games. There were two competitions at the time: the league and the Copa Colombia, the latter, organized in the likes of the English FA Cup, was little more than an attempt to increase revenues. The dates of the Copa Colombia, as a second-tier tournament, often clashed with important friendly matches.

There are 24 doubleheaders in the dataset, meaning that four teams played sequentially on the same day at the same stadium. It occurs for two main reasons. First, to maximize profits by drawing large attendances. Such is the case, for instance, with the inauguration of the Atanasio Girardot stadium in Medellin in March 1953, which hosted three doubleheaders featuring Atlético Nacional, Deportivo Cali, Alianza Lima (PER), and Fluminense (BRA).

A second reason is to aid in the survival of teams with financial difficulties, all too often during this period. An example is the June 1952 league match between Universidad and Junior, which took place before the grand friendly game between Millonarios and Flamengo (BRA). In some extreme cases, the same club played both matches. It happened, for instance, on August 3, 1952, when Millonarios defeated Sporting in matchday 11 of the league competition and later that day overpowered Botafogo 4-1 in an international friendly. A few days later, on August 12, Cali replicated Millonarios' feat, drawing with Austria Vienna 1-1 after defeating Cúcuta 3-2 in an official league game. Once accounting for doubleheaders, the dataset contains attendance data for 700 games and revenue information for 421 matchdays.

The main competition was the league, debuting in 1948. The stars, however, arrived a year later. In 1949, the league began in May, but Pedernera did not make his debut until June, when Millonarios was second, tied with Santa Fe, just two points behind Deportivo Cali. Rossi and Di Stéfano made their debut on matchday 14, on August 14, in Bogota against Deportivo Barranquilla. At the time, the team was two points behind Cali thanks to a recent 1–3 win in Cali, a match that generated revenues of COP 90,000 (USD 45,918). Before 18,000 fans, against Barranquilla, Rossi displayed a "perfect positioning" and "mathematical passing", Pedernera achieved "the highest expression of intelligence in the exclusive service of association football", and Di Stéfano, who scored the first of Millonarios' five goals, showed that his "speed and mobility on the pitch make him extremely dangerous".[227]

In six of the next seven games, Millonarios scored five goals, missing only in the victory against Boca Juniors in Bogota before 15,000 fans. Then, on August 9, came a bizarre game against América in Bogota. Two of América's Colombian stars, Roaldo Viáfara and Saulo Flórez, had been imposed a game ban earlier that week. Manuel Correa Valencia, Dimayor's vice-president, and America's President, no doubt worried about the five-goal streak, claimed that without Viáfara and Flórez the team "was no match for Millonarios".[228] To satisfy the 10,000 fans already inside the stadium, Correa signed a letter conceding Millonarios the two points, but convinced everyone to play a friendly match. Millonarios, relaxed, lost 1–2, but it turns out, fans thought the game was for real. Only when the game was over did everyone find out that it had been a friendly.[229] After the natural scandal, Millonarios ultimately won because América played with two banned players.

Millonarios kept on winning, with 30,000 fans attending a 3–6 against Santa Fe and then an additional five against Universidad (10,000 fans) in two away games. The league would be decided in a match between Cali and Millonarios in Bogota. Given that Millonarios' game against Medellín in Bogota was postponed, a draw or a win against Cali would give the Bogota team its first league title.

23,000 attended El Campín on November 6, 1949, with both teams on top of the table with 42 points. While Millonarios complained about the uneven, muddy pitch due to the heavy rain, Cali forced up to 14 corners, winning by two goals from Valeriano and Barbadillo.[230] Days later, Millonarios defeated Medellín, forcing Dimayor to organize a two-leg final between Cali and Millonarios. In the first game, Di Stéfano scored a penalty kick to give Millonarios a 0–1 victory, and with over 25,000 fans at El Campín, Millonarios defeated Cali 3-2 in the second leg. Counting América's game, Millonarios won 23 out of 26 games, scored 103 goals (five or more in 13 games). Santa Fe, which finished third that season, scored 101 goals. The differences between early investors and the rest were significant, allowing the top teams to thrash their opponents in many games.

The first edition of the Copa Colombia started in October 1950 and did not finish until February 1951, with Boca Juniors celebrating after defeating Santa Fe 4-2 in Cali and losing 4-3 in Bogota.

In the league, Millonarios could not revalidate its 1949 title, surprisingly losing to Caldas in 1950. Millonarios arrived as leaders and undefeated to visit Deportivo Cali for matchday 13 on May 21. The 14,845 fans that left revenues of COP 57,042 (USD 22,725) enjoyed a surprising 6-1 Millonarios defeat, their biggest loss during El Dorado. Higgins, the former Everton player made his debut that fateful day but complained that he had been injured since minute ten, when Cabillón replaced him; by then, the game was 4-1.[231] Valeriano, the Peruvian superstar, marked the difference, playing one of his best games in Colombia. He scored three goals and assisted two more.

Millonarios lost four games that season. After the loss in Cali, the Bogota side won only twice in their next seven games, losing three and drawing two. By matchday 25 on August 20, Deportes Caldas could even afford to lose at home in Manizales—2–3 against Millonarios before a record crowd of 12,000—and still remained leaders.

Deportes Caldas was a formidable rival for Millonarios in that 1950 season. In November, in Copa Colombia, Caldas drew 3-3 with Millonarios in Bogota. After 15 minutes, Caldas was winning 1–2. In the 30th minute, a challenge between two Argentines, Aves (Millonarios) and Ávila (Caldas), inside the Millonarios' box resulted in the latter rolling on the grass, and the Caldas players demanded a penalty kick from the Italian referee Diego de Leo. Denying the foul sparked a reaction from some Caldas players that bordered on savagery. With Ávila still on the ground, Tesori walked up to the referee and struck him square in the face. Players from both teams surrounded the Italian, some throwing blows, others trying to separate and protect the referee, until the police restored order. Once free, De Leo sent off Tesori, Navarro, Luengo, and Padín. Caldas continued with eight players because, although the referee, who refused to continue officiating, had expelled four, Millonarios allowed one to remain on the pitch. Caldas held firm and even added a third goal through Ávila. Millonarios, stunned and humiliated, pushed forward, managing to equalize through Aguilera and Di Stéfano.[232] Three days later, in Manizales, they drew again, 3-3, and it was not until the next day that Caldas eliminated Millonarios from the Copa Colombia, winning the match 3-2.

True that in nine days, Millonarios had played four games, having drawn with Hungaria on November 19, and that not all regular players played in Manizales, but there is no question that Caldas was a significant rival for Millonarios in 1950.

Caldas did not play further in that version of the Copa Colombia because most players' contracts had been finalized by the end of the year, and, unable to renew them in time, it could not guarantee a competitive roster before the finals, played in February 1951.

The following edition had to wait until April 1952 to start, a Copa Colombia that Millonarios won, but whose final took place in 1953. In October 1952, Cúcuta had no answer for Millonarios. The first leg of the semifinal between the best of Uruguay and Argentina finished with the latter's 1–2 victory in front of 10,000 spectators, who left COP 23,000 (USD 9,163). A month later, in Bogota, 13,000 fans saw Millonarios defeat Cúcuta 2-1. Fans had to wait until May 1953 to see the final match of the Copa Colombia, when Millonarios defeated Boca Juniors 3-0, recovering from a 2-0 loss in Cali. The best days of El Dorado coincide with the best days of Millonarios, the winner of the league in 1951, 1952, and 1953.

In the 1951 league, Millonarios scored 60 points, leaving runner-up Boca Juniors 11 points behind. That season, Millonarios lost two games, one to Junior in Bogota and the other in Cucuta, 2-1, with an attendance of 18,000 spectators, generating revenues of COP 35,421 (USD 14,112). In contrast, Millonarios reached five or more goals six times in 34 matches, including a 7–0 thrashing of Nacional in Medellin and home wins of five goals apiece against Santa Fe and Boca Juniors. Each of the latter two games, played in October, left gate receipts of around COP 68,000 (USD 27,091).

Cúcuta defeated Millonarios late in the season, but for some time, the Uruguayans seemed like a genuine alternative to the domain of Pedernera and company. After the first eight matches, Millonarios was on top with 15 points, just two ahead of Cúcuta. Before the game between the first and second, fans traveled by land and air. Twenty-two thousand fans attended the game in the stadium of Universidad Nacional, paying a total of COP 89,475 (USD 35,647) to see a Pedernera header and a 35-meter unstoppable shot, and a bicycle kick goal by Di Stéfano to finish in a 3-0 defeat for Cúcuta.[233]

Millonarios won the 1951 league, but Boca Juniors scored 112 goals, 15 more than the Bogota club, thanks to nine games with five or more goals, including 10 against Nacional in Medellin and 9 against Huracán in Cali. Millonarios, however, humbled them in both legs.

In 1952, with Boca Juniors again as runner-up, Millonarios repeated as champion. It did not begin strongly, with three draws in the first six games, but it won the big games against Boca Juniors (0–2), Santa Fe (6-0), and Pereira (5-0), which would finish third that season. Millonarios managed an undefeated streak of 17 games, losing 1-0 in Pereira in front of 12,000 excited fans. The title, however, was never in danger.

The 1953 league finished with Millonarios just two points ahead of Quindío, and four points ahead of Boca Juniors. Although the latter only won a Copa Colombia, and despite its perpetual financial issues, it was arguably the second-best domestic team during El Dorado. The game between the two was a top derby; however, the Cali team only managed to defeat Millonarios in their first match in May 1949. In 1950, two draws gave Caldas the title, but from 1951 onward, Boca Juniors lost all games. Matches between Millonarios and Boca—including friendlies—drew an average of 18,100 spectators, based on attendance figures from 12 of the 15 games played between 1949 and 1953.

Despite its performance, Boca Juniors was not the most significant rival to Millonarios. Its games against Cali (based on data from 14 out of 19 matches) drew an average of 20,350. It was, however, with Santa Fe the main rivalry as measured by attendance: 26,033 on average (15/17). These figures contrast with the Cali versus Santa Fe game, which averaged 12,266 fans (13/22); Santa Fe versus Boca Juniors, which averaged 14,247 (7/16); and Cali versus Boca, averaging 10,100 (6/18).

At the time, friendlies played an important role. In the absence of club international official competitions, such as the Copa Libertadores, friendly games were a significant revenue source and the only way to compare with international peers. In Colombia, before being expelled from FIFA and after the Lima Agreement, domestic teams invested in bringing clubs, while also traveling abroad, primarily to South and Central America.

Figure 2.1 depicts the available attendance per semester, segmented by friendlies and official matches. Attendance, of course, is limited by the available infrastructure. On average, stadiums had limited capacity, and some, such as El Campín, underwent restoration. The Bogota stadium was closed from

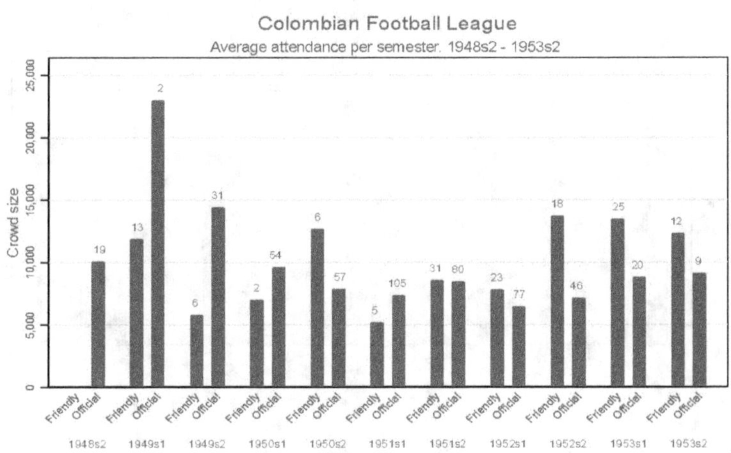


*Figure 2.1* Average attendance, 1948–1953

early 1951 to July 1952. Millonarios, Santa Fe, and Universidad played at the smaller Alfonso López stadium on the National University campus.

Based on the reported maximum attendance, it is possible to estimate each stadium's potential capacity. However, these figures may, in some cases, reflect the reporter's subjective view and, most significantly, attendance above the stadium's nominal capacity. El Campín in Bogota, for instance, could potentially host around 50,000 fans. In Cali, the Pascual Guerrero received over 25,000 supporters in some games. In Medellin, the figure was around 12,000–15,000 fans for the old San Fernando horse racetrack and 35,000 for the new Atanasio Girardot, while the Municipal stadium in Barranquilla could accommodate around 13,000 supporters. In the remaining cities, the largest were the San José Stadium in Armenia, with a capacity of over 20,000 fans, and General Santander in Cucuta (18,000), followed by those in Bucaramanga, Pereira, and Manizales, which hosted around 10,000–12,000 fans each.

Given the overall capacity, the average attendance of over 10,000 per game is respectable, though not overwhelming. Official games averaged 10,215 spectators per game, friendlies 9,923.

Still, the 10,000 figure is smaller than that registered in historical footballing countries such as Argentina or England. Figure 2.2 compares Colombian attendance data with English and scattered data from Argentina. The difference in attendance is notorious. Of course, by 1950, many stadiums in England were over 50 years old, while in Colombia, some cities, such as Medellin, had no football stadiums. In England, the average attendance is about 3.5 times that in Colombia.

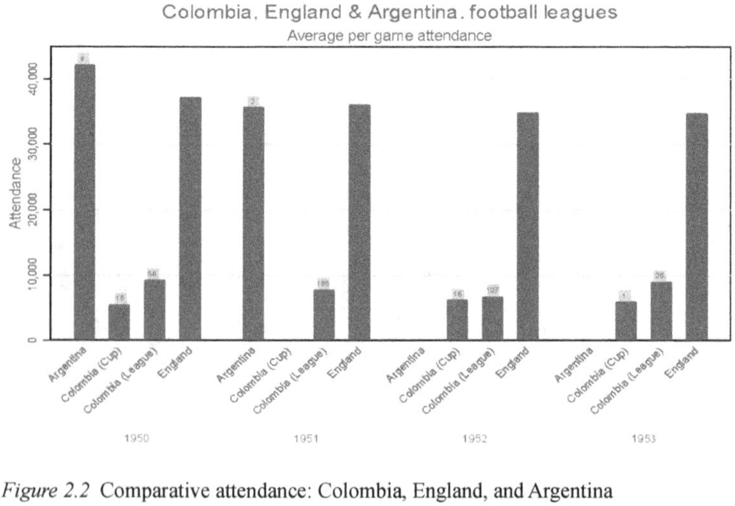


*Figure 2.2* Comparative attendance: Colombia, England, and Argentina

With lower attendance figures than its peers, it might be that ticket prices were higher. Revenues in Colombia between 1948 and 1953, as depicted in Figure 2.3, average COP 20,848 (USD 9,399) per game, a sizable figure.

The numbers in Figure 2.3 must be interpreted with care when data are scarce, because press reports tend to focus on the most significant games. In 1949, for instance, there are gate receipts records for just three official games, all for Millonarios, including the derby against Santa Fe (COP 57,000—USD 29,081) and a visitor game versus Cali (COP 90,000 – USD 45,918). After matchday 9, Deportivo Cali led the league with 16 points, followed by Millonarios and Santa Fe with 14 points, and Medellín in fourth with 12.

On July 10, Millonarios and Santa Fe drew 2-2 in a packed El Campín stadium, where 30,000 left revenues of COP 57,000 (USD 29,081). A week later, Millonarios played away in Medellin, beating the Danza del Sol 1–6, with a record of COP 20,000 (USD 7,968). On July 31, 2,000 fans flew from Bogota to Cali to watch the game with Deportivo Cali. Cali, undefeated, led the league with 21 points, two more than Millonarios. With a 1–3 victory and record gate receipts of COP 90,000 (USD 35,856), Millonarios laid the foundations for their first league title.

There are, however, enough observations for official games between the first semester of 1950 and the second semester of 1952, revealing that the average gate receipts per game (officials and friendlies) were a sizable COP 18,298 (USD 7,290). Moreover, gate receipts for official games (Figure 2.3), covering 93 of 350 games, confirm that the peak of El Dorado was in 1951, with an average gate receipt per match of COP 20,000 (USD 9,302).

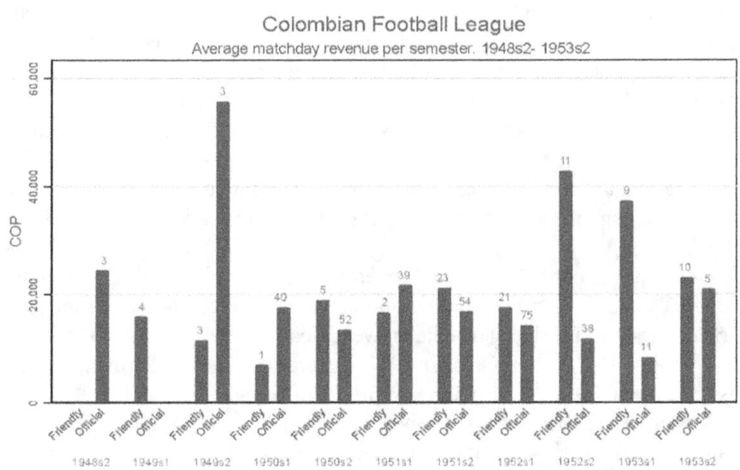


*Figure 2.3* Average gate receipts per match, 1948–1953

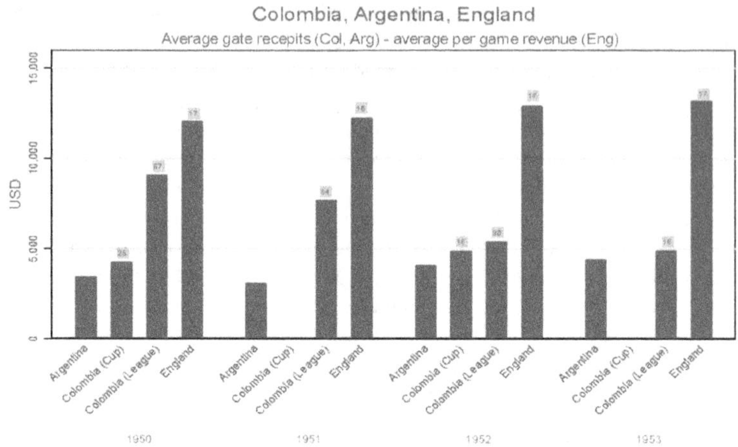


*Figure 2.4* A comparison of average gate receipts

Figure 2.4 compares gate receipts figures for official games in Colombia with those available in England and Argentina. Between 1950 and 1952, Colombia's revenue was clearly above Argentina's, though the gap narrowed in 1952 and disappeared in 1953. The gate receipts figures in England are larger than in Colombia, but while they remain relatively stable in the former, they have a clear downward pattern in the latter.

Revenues in Colombia were indeed relatively higher during the initial days of El Dorado. In 1950, the ratio of GDP per capita between England and Colombia was roughly 3 to 1, and between Argentina and Colombia was approximately 2.1 to 1. Yet, gate receipts in England were only 32% larger than in Colombia that year, and Colombian league revenues were, on average, 160% higher than in Argentina. These gate receipt ratios narrowed over time, approaching the GDP per capita ratios by 1953 and, in the case of Argentina, nearly disappearing altogether. Neil Franklin was right. In England, footballers were making the big bucks for others. In Colombia, following Senior's concepts, using the money to pay for the best, they managed to build a unique league.

As already mentioned, football revenues came from official and friendly games. The latter were financially important and a source of much of the historical epic of El Dorado. The epic, however, came after FIFA lifted the sanctions against Dimayor in October 1951. Before that, mostly Peruvian teams visited Colombia, as did a small team from Rio de Janeiro, Madureira.

Madureira, it turns out, is a good example of the quality change Colombian football experienced. The Brazilians toured Colombia between February and March 1949. They played seven games against Junior, Millonarios, and Santa Fe, leaving the country undefeated, conceding only three draws.

The same team played another five games against Colombian clubs in March 1952. It lost four games to Quindío, Millonarios, and Boca Juniors. Although seven days later, Millonarios won 3-0, Madureira's only win was a 2–5 over Millonarios in their second game in the country. For the Bogota club, it was the culmination of a disappointing international tour in Bolivia and Uruguay. Days earlier, in February, playing in a friendly cup in Venezuela, Quindío won 3-2 in its first game against Madureira, losing 1–3 days later. Sporting, also competing in that tournament, defeated the Brazilians 3-2. The progress of the Colombian clubs was apparent.

During the ban, between November 1949 and October 1951, Colombian teams played only 32 games against foreign teams. Cali successfully toured Central America and Ecuador, undefeated in 7 games, until it met its neighbor, Boca Juniors, in December 1950.

In July 1951, Santa Fe played and won three games in La Paz, scoring 13 goals and conceding just three, with a reported attendance of 15,000 spectators per match in its first two games. Earlier, in February, Millonarios also toured Bolivia, playing four games, but winning only two. It drew 3-3 against Bolívar (BOL) and a combination of Bolivian players. Eighteen thousand fans attended Millonarios' debut victory against Bolívar 1–3.

Mainly, rogue teams visited the country during this period. Hungaria played eight games in Colombia, losing all but two. On November 19, 1950, they drew 1-1 with Millonarios at El Campín, followed by a remarkable 5-5 draw against Libertad in Barranquilla a month later. It lost two games to Santa Fe and one apiece to Cúcuta, Millonarios, Medellín, and Boca Juniors. The Hungarians scored 18 goals in Colombia, conceding 29, including five in each game against Millonarios, Santa Fe, Libertad, and Medellín.

Wanders did not perform very well either. In seven games, they only won in Medellin, 1–5 on January 28, 1951, which, according to one of its players, Urruti, was the key game because the owners of Quindío saw it, and it was then that they decided to hire the entire team for the league's debut season. Wanders managed to draw with Cúcuta and lost the rest of the games, scoring 15 goals and conceding 21.

There was a significant upgrade in the quality of the international rivals following the Lima Pact. Sport Boys (PER) and Universidad de Chile (CHI) came between November and December 1951. The Peruvians made their debut on November 23, losing 5-3 against Cali in a rainy, muddy game with 8,000 fans paying COP 12,355 (USD 4,922). Then came Millonarios in Bogota, where 15,000 entered El Campín expecting a load of goals.

Millonarios played with its legendary lineup: Cozzi, Pini, Zuluaga, Ramírez, Rossi, Soria, Reyes, Pedernera, Di Stéfano, Báez, Mourin. Sport Boys, the current Peruvian champion, had among its players Barbadillo and Valeriano López, former stars in Colombia. Against all odds, Millonarios lost 0–1, unable to equalize the Barbadillo goal in the 19th minute of the first half. Excuses were abundant: the ultra-defensive Peruvian strategy, Millonarios shooting many times but missing once and again, Pedernera injured, or the referee disallowing a Di Stéfano goal for a "non-existent" offside. Millonarios asked for a rematch; the Peruvians initially agreed, then set a condition that the game be in Lima, and finally rejected any further matches.

In the 1951 Colombian tour, Sport Boys won two games (Millonarios and América), but also conceded five goals in each of its losses against Pereira and Cali. In 1952, they played three games in Lima against Cali (a 2-2 draw in front of 30,000 fans), Cúcuta, and Universidad. The Cúcuta's Uruguayans humbled them 1–7.

In December 1951, Universidad Católica (CHI) scraped a draw against Boca Juniors in Quito but lost all three matches in Colombia—four goals to Junior, and five apiece to Santa Fe in both encounters.

The main dish of the 1951–1952 international season was San Lorenzo (ARG) and Racing (ARG), the triple Argentine league champion (1949, 1950, and 1951). San Lorenzo made its debut, losing to Cali 2-1 on December 2, 1951, in front of 15,000, who generated revenues of COP 30,748 (USD 12,250). It played and won two games in Barranquilla, where Junior lost 0–2 and 0–7. San Lorenzo lost to Millonarios 1-0, with 12,000 fans for gate receipts of COP 18,000 (USD 7,171). Santa Fe played San Lorenzo twice. With 18,000 fans and gate receipts of COP 50,000 (USD 19,920), it defeated the Argentines 4-2. With Chamorro, Miotti, Martínez, Dokú, Perucca, Benegas, Moyano, Fernández, Pontoni, Rial, and Contreras, Santa Fe played one "of the best games of the past years".[234] On December 30, playing with the same lineup except for Dokú, replaced by Arnaldo, Santa Fe lost 4–8. With no other explanation, maybe the holidays took a toll on the then-called "Santos" stars.

San Lorenzo played seven games against Colombian teams, winning three and drawing 2. It played an eighth game in Bogota against Racing. Only 6,000 fans attended the game (COP 8,000—USD 3,187). At the time, the main attractions were the local teams, which explains why the debut of Racing against Millonarios drew 40,000 fans to El Campín, setting a record of COP 107,000 (USD 42,629).

The injury Pedernera claimed in the game against Sport Boys must have been real, since he did not play in the first match against Racing. The best possible Millonarios lineup included Castillo instead of Pedernera. The first half finished 2-2, including a bicycle kick goal by Di Stéfano. The game remained tied until the last minute, when Di Stéfano scored the winning goal, 4-3 for the Colombian champions versus the Argentines.

The rematch came two days later, with Millonarios now fielding Pedernera. Twenty-eight thousand fans that left revenues of COP 75,000 (USD 29,880) saw the Argentines lose again, this time 2-0, thanks to two goals from Báez. At the time, with its tactics in mind, Pedernera was stating that "Millonarios is the best team in America".[235] In Argentina, they adopted that phrase and, given the performance against the Argentines, expectations grew for seeing Pedernera and company in Buenos Aires. Unfortunately, that test never happened.

Racing also played and drew twice with Cali and played three more with Santa Fe. The first game in Cali drew 10,000 fans and generated revenue of COP 34,977 (USD 13,895), while the second game against Santa Fe, with 20,000 fans, generated revenue of COP 52,000 (USD 20,717). Santa Fe drew the first game, lost the second, but won 5-4 in the third, almost blowing a 5-1 lead. In its last match in Colombia, Racing lost before 4,000 fans against Junior in Barranquilla, generating revenues of COP 18,000 (USD 7,171). Racing, which lost four games, drew three, and won just two, attracted an average of 14,400 spectators per game, generating per-match revenues of COP 43,500 (USD 17,330). Friendlies were, indeed, good business.

In February 1952, Quindío and Sporting participated in the *Copa Ministerio de Defensa* in Caracas. Quindío championed, winning four games, drawing one (to Sporting), and losing the aforementioned match against Madureira. Sporting finished third, losing only to Quindío, but scored fewer goals than Madureira, second. Sporting also played on December 23 against Banfield (ARG). The Colombians won 4-2 in Barranquilla, where the 6,800 fans generated revenue of COP 18,000 (USD 7,171).

Between February and March 1952, Santa Fe toured Ecuador, Guatemala, and El Salvador. In Quito, in front of 25,000 and 15,000 fans, respectively, they played and lost twice against Boca Juniors, then moved to Guayaquil, drawing twice against Río Guayas (ECU) and defeating Everest (ECU) 3–4. As detailed later on, the tour's objective was to raise funds to pay the players before releasing them. Not the best scenario for optimal performance. Still, the team's quality was superior to that of any Central American team, and they won five of six games.

Cali was one of the most active teams. Between January and March 1952, it played three games in Brazil, two in Chile, four in Lima, and two in Guayaquil. In Brazil, it lost to Flamengo 4-1, drew in São Paulo against a combination of Palmeiras and São Paulo players, and defeated Ponte Preta 3–4. Overall, it won seven games, drew three, and lost only that match against Flamengo. The tour was a success, scoring 31 goals and conceding only 22. The other Cali powerhouse, Boca Juniors, toured Guatemala between February and March. They played six games, losing only one against Comunicaciones de Guatemala 2-1, and winning the other five, scoring 25 goals and conceding five.

With Pedernera orchestrating, Di Stéfano and "Pipo" Rossi starring, and four titles in five seasons, Millonarios became the flagship of El Dorado. The roster was expensive, and the club had to play constantly to pay its stars. Millonarios was a valued team across the Americas, charging USD 5,000 per game, more than the USD 4,000 Racing charged during its Colombian tour. Too many games had a toll.

Millonarios' last game of the 1951 season was on December 23 in Bogota, beating San Lorenzo 1-0. Exactly one month later, on January 23, 1952, they were in Chile, defeating Audax Italiano 0–1 in front of 50,000 enthusiastic Chileans. Between that first match and the last friendly of the preseason,

70 days passed during which the team played 16 games, including Bolivia, Colombia, Chile, Spain, and Uruguay. One game every 4,38 days, with the caveat that there were no direct flight connections. A typical trip to Buenos Aires would require stops in Lima and Santiago de Chile. Overall, Millonarios spend much of their preparation time at airports.

In January and February 1952, Millonarios played three games in Santiago and one in Viña del Mar. On average, 48,000 fans attended the former, 19,100 the latter. The Colombians won two and drew two before flying to La Paz, where, within 24 hours of arrival, they lost 2-1 to Bolívar. If one seeks a pattern, Pedernera left the pitch just fifteen minutes in—though not before scoring Millonarios' only goal.

Then came Nacional and Peñarol, the two powerhouses of Uruguay, the current FIFA World Champions. It was a big opportunity for Millonarios to write their name with golden letters in the books of football history. Their debut, however, was a 0–0 draw against the smaller side, River Plate (URU).

Millonarios, with 35,000 fans in the stands, played a great match against Nacional. Pedernera gave the lead in the first half. Five minutes into the second half, the referee sent Rossi to the showers and awarded Nacional a penalty kick, which they converted. With the Uruguayans pushing hard, the referee sent off Báez, leaving Millonarios with nine players. Souto scored the second and final goal for Nacional at minute 33.

A couple of days later, 45,000 fans arrived to see Peñarol and Millonarios. Stemberg played instead of Ramírez for Millonarios. Peñarol was the backbone of the Uruguayan team that defeated Brazil at the Maracanã in 1950. Roque Gastón Maspoli, the goalkeeper; Obdulio Varela, the center-half; and the two scorers in that historic match, Juan Alberto Schiaffino and Alcides Ghiggia.

No one was sent off, but Millonarios lost 2-1 again. Vidal scored for Peñarol early in the game, but Aguilera, who had entered in substitution of Mourín for the second half, scored the equalizer. In the 33rd minute, as in the match against Nacional, Peñarol scored via Juan Eduardo Hohberg. Despite their two defeats, Millonarios left Uruguay with the impression of being a great side, let down only by poor finishing. A picture that contradicts its legend. Millonarios returned to Bogota for two matches against Madureira before, ten days later, debuting on the Spanish tour that would definitely place their name in history.

On February 15, 1952, Santiago Bernabéu for Real Madrid and Alfonso Senior for Millonarios signed a contract in Madrid under which Millonarios would play five games in Spain, including the cup commemorating the 50th birthday of Real Madrid. Millonarios charged nothing, having the Spaniards pay the USD 35,000 bill for hosting the team.[236] In exchange, Real committed to playing five games in Colombia, and one can assume that Millos would pay that bill. In practice, the Spaniards only played two games in Colombia, plus two additional games against Millonarios in Caracas in the *Copa Coronel Marcos Pérez Jiménez*.

Millonarios flew 20 players in two groups via New York, Lisboa, and Madrid, including Santa Fe player Jorge Benegas as reinforcement. On March 19, 1952, a Colombian club played its first game on European soil. Cozzi, Pini, Zuluaga, Ramírez, Rossi, Soría, Castillo, Pedernera, Di Stéfano, Báez, and Mourín played and drew 0-0 against Valencia in front of 25,000 supporters. According to Di Stéfano's biography, the referee called a corner kick a clear penalty on him.[237] It was the beginning of long travel hours across Spanish territory. Di Stéfano claims that it took the bus 9.5 hours to travel from Madrid to Valencia, where no hotels were available. They had to stay in a large family's house.[238] Despite the result in Valencia, the Spanish press began to notice Di Stéfano, of whom they wrote: "he quickly moves from the center of the pitch to find space, forcing his marker to abandon his position and leave the middle of the defense exposed".[239]

The difference in style was notorious. Jacinto, Valencia player, complained that "they did a nice game but excessively abused passing the ball" ... tiki taka was decades away.[240] Asensi, in some sense, confirmed the impression: "the five forwards are great, what a way to lose the markers, but they scarcely shoot".[241] Marca wrote about the Valencia match that

> the Colombians play horizontally too much, they do not enter the area frequently, and shoot from a long distance. However, when they accelerate, they are very dangerous, and the forwards easily lose their markers, moving between positions to confuse the defenders.[242]

On March 26, after an eight-hour flight to the Canary Islands, they lost 3-2 against Las Palmas, relegated to the second division at the end of that season. Millonarios fielded the best players, except for Danilo replacing Pini. Starting the game, the 30,000 fans saw Cozzi cut a cross but lose control of the ball when trying to clear it. Gallardo had but to push the ball to the net. Despite a second Las Palmas goal, Millonarios kept control of the game, passing the ball continuously with just a few shots.

In the second half, Millonarios leveled through Reyes and Di Stéfano, the latter after dribbling past several Spanish players. A few minutes later, Las Palmas scored the third goal. Another defeat for Millonarios in a game they controlled but failed to put away. Zuluaga, the only Colombian in Millonarios' starting eleven, had to leave injured his position at 40 minutes of the first half. He would not play more in Spain.

The third game was the first of the 50th anniversary of Real Madrid. By then, Norrköping officials were saying that they would defeat Millonarios, "a less dangerous rival than the host, Real Madrid".[243] Confidence in Colombia was low, facing a club that was about to win its sixth Swedish league in ten years. Forty thousand fans attended Real Madrid's stadium to watch the game.

Missing Zuluaga, Millonarios fielded the best it had with Stemberg next to Pini in the defensive line. Millonarios controlled the ball and the game on a muddy pitch in the rain, but, almost as usual, it failed to score and turn its dominance into goals. Thus, in the 39th minute, Kallgren shot, and depending on who you believe, either the shot was unstoppable, or Cozzi failed to grab the ball. Either way, Millonarios was losing again. It took Báez 26 minutes of the second half to level the game. An own goal, just 8 minutes away from the end, put Millonarios in the lead. However, Norrköping scored the final 2-2 just a minute later.

On March 30, 1952, Millonarios defeated Real Madrid 2–4 in a packed Chamartín Stadium with 70,000 fans. Millonarios controlled the game, as they had in many games before, but this time they hit the target. ABC, the Madrid newspaper, wrote about the elegance and quality of Pedernera and colleagues:

> The class of Millonarios is beyond dispute [...] A true spectator, he who genuinely follows the game is unlikely ever to feel let down. Because win or lose, Millonarios will produce numerous passages of play throughout the match that amount to pure exhibition, to delicate craftsmanship [...] In this Colombian football, there are no wild hacks or even long clearances.[244]

Millonarios played with the best it had available: Cozzi, captain; given Zuluaga's absence, Benegas, Pini, Ramírez, Rossi, Soria, Castillo, Pedernera, Báez, and Mourín. The South Americans controlled the first half with Castillo scoring within 18 minutes into the game. Di Stéfano and then Pedernera scored two more before the first half was over.

The second half began as the first had finished, with Millonarios scoring, Castillo assisting to Di Stéfano. The Ambassadors, as they were already known, held a four-goal lead, but the kilometers in their legs began to tell. Real Madrid pulled one back 15 minutes into the second half, then added a second 15 minutes later.

Millonarios won fairly, but the Madrid press still had time to complain about the referee. For a team that had never been in Spain, it is surprising to read that the referee was favoring the Colombians. ABC wrote: "The referee contributed to Madrid's disorder. (...) Rossi, ungainly and disagreeable, capable of every foul the referee will let him get away with—on every occasion—but a magnificent player and enormously active".[245]

The last Spanish match took place the day after the victory in Madrid. Millonarios was about to play its fourth game in six days. Unable to fly because the airport in Seville was closed due to weather conditions, the team took a train to Andalucia at 8:30 a.m. Pini, Zuluaga, and Danilo, the defense and their substitute, were injured and stayed in Madrid. The lineup had only six traditional starters, and not all of them in their natural positions: Cozzi, Ramírez, Benegas, Soria, Rossi y González, Castillo, Mosquera, Di Stéfano, Mourín y Aguilera. Still, a packed stadium with 30,000 fans saw Rossi miss a penalty in the 32nd minute. Later in the game, in the 38th minute, Di Stéfano scored a free kick. Sevilla (ESP) equalized nine minutes into the second half.

The Spanish tour was a success, with an average attendance of 39,000 eager fans to watch the South American stars. Di Stéfano was the goalscorer, with five goals, and the player who caught the Spanish press and clubs' attention. As early as April 2, Samitier, representing Barcelona, expressed the Catalans' interest in Di Stéfano. Simultaneously, Real Madrid was trying to have him play for Madrid for three months, just after the end of Colombia's season. It was the beginning of arguably the most important transfer process of the twentieth century.

Friendly season came back fast: in June, Millonarios played Flamengo (BRA). It defeated them 4-1 in Bogota with 40,000 fans that left COP 80,000 (USD 31,872). Flamengo flew and drew with Cali 1-1 before 15,000 spectators, then defeated Quindío in Armenia, where 4,000 generated revenues of COP 12,000 (USD 4,780). Boca Juniors also played Flamengo, but in Ecuador, where 30,000 saw the Brazilians win 6-3.

A note on USD 4,780 generated in Armenia. We have no information on how much Flamengo charged per game, but Racing's fee was around USD 4,000, and Millonarios' USD 5,000. For comparison, Sevilla demanded USD 6,500 to play in Bogota during their Colombian tour—a figure swiftly rejected—and then turned down USD 12,000 for three games in the capital. We also know that Cali charged USD 3,500 per match for their 1952 Peruvian tour. One could argue, given the figures, that gate receipts under USD 5,000 may not have been enough to make these high-end friendlies worthwhile.

During the mid-year break, Cúcuta also traveled to Ecuador, winning two of three games and defeating Pereira 4-3 in a match played in Guayaquil. They went on to play in Peru, winning both games, including the aforementioned 1–7 victory over Sport Boys. Pereira played four additional games in Ecuador. Not only did the big clubs draw fans, but smaller sides did as well in foreign lands. Fifteen thousand fans attended Pereira's 0–3 victory against Barcelona (ECU) in Guayaquil.

The core of this mid-year friendly season was the Brazilians, including Flamengo and Botafogo (BRA), the exotic visits of Austria Vienna (AUT) and Sevilla, and, of course, Real Madrid. In their first game, Botafogo defeated Millonarios 1–2 in Bogota on July 13, 1952. 35,000 disappointed fans brought in COP 110,000 (USD 43,824). The Brazilians defeated Universidad 0–1 days later in front of 12,000 fans, before inflicting a humiliating 3-0 defeat on Millonarios in Caracas in the *Copa Coronel Marcos Pérez Jiménez*.

In the second game of the *Copa* in Caracas, Millonarios managed to control the Brazilians, drawing 4-4, and finally defeated them 4-1 a week later in Bogota before 29,300 fans who generated revenues of COP 85,000 (USD 33,864).

Austria Viena played seven games in Colombia, losing 3-2 in their debut against Santa Fe before 15,000, with a gate of COP 49,000 (USD 19,521). The Austrians drew 1-1 with Universidad in front of 7,200 fans, humiliated

Atlético Nacional, 1–9 in Medellin, and then lost 2-1 to Millonarios with just 6,000 spectators. After the Spanish tour, during a short league break in May, Millonarios lost 4-1 to Boca Juniors in Ecuador and 1-0 to Barcelona (ECU). The team was playing a game every 4,75 days. Austria drew its last three games, one in Cucuta and two against Cali, the last of which drew 23,00 fans, generating revenue of COP 45,000 (USD 17,928).

Sevilla drew 1-1 in its debut on July 20 in Cali against Boca Juniors in front of 16,000 spectators that paid a total of COP 33,000 (USD 13,147). They played three additional matches, drawing with Cali, losing 3-0 to Cúcuta, and finishing with a 4-4 draw against América.

In the summer of 1952, Millonarios and Real Madrid played four games: two in Bogota and two in the *Copa* in Caracas. On July 6, 55,000 fans squeezed into El Campín, leaving a record COP 140,000 (USD 55,776). Millonarios fielded its historical lineup. Olsen, the Argentine who had arrived from Racing, scored the first goal for Real Madrid. Fifteen minutes into the second half, Reyes crossed from the right, Báez flicked the ball with his head, leaving Alonso, the goalkeeper, with nothing but air in his hands, and Di Stéfano pushed the ball smoothly into the goal. In the 37th minute, Mourín dribbled past the defender, sent a short pass to Di Stéfano, who let the ball pass by to Pedernera, scoring the winning goal.

Bogota was living a dream, making it natural to have a rematch between Millonarios and Real Madrid, just three days after the demonstration of the first game. The match took place on a Wednesday at 12:15 p.m., forcing many firms and businesses to adjust their working hours so fans could attend the stadium, and public transportation to reorganize its routes to meet the demand. Prices for the game ranged between COP 1.5 (USD 0.6) and COP 6 (USD 2.4), the latter not cheap considering that the minimum wage was COP 60 (USD 24).

Third game, third victory for Millonarios, but this time, the Spanish deserved more in a game with more tension and aggressiveness. At the 32nd minute of the second half, after a clash between Zuluaga and Joseíto and the resulting scrum, the referee sent off Zuluaga and Oliva, leaving each team with ten men. Báez, in the 9th minute of the first half, scored the sole goal with a long-distance shot, and the referee canceled a Real Madrid goal for offside. Three days later, Millonarios lost to Botafogo and then flew to Caracas to play Real Madrid again. That made four games in ten days.

In Caracas, Millonarios dispatched La Salle (VEN) with ease but drew 1-1 with Real Madrid in both matches. Rossi and Di Stéfano scored the respective goals. Real Madrid also drew both games with Botafogo. The Spanish won the *Copa Coronel Marcos Pérez Jiménez* under a goal-average rule that divided the number of goals scored by the number of goals conceded. Real Madrid: 1.857; Botafogo: 1.667. Millonarios finished third, one point behind. Three days after the last match in Venezuela, Millonarios defeated Botafogo in Bogota.

1952 finished with another grand friendly season that lasted into January and February. River Plate (ARG), Boca Juniors (ARG), Independiente (ARG), and Huracán (ARG) flew from Argentina. Alianza Lima (PER) and Fluminense (BRA) joined Rapid Vienna (AUT).

Boca Juniors (ARG) won two games and lost two against Quindío and Santa Fe. The former attracted 5,000 fans and generated revenue of COP 13,000 (USD 5,179), while the latter, held in Bogota, drew 18,000 spectators.

Independiente also had mixed results in its five games. Playing between February and March 1953, they initially lost to the two Cali teams (Cali and Boca Juniors), recovering in Pereira (before 4,000 fans) and Cali (5,000 fans), winning 0–4 in both games. Its last match, in Bogota before 8,000 fans, resulted in a 3-2 win for Santa Fe.

Huracán played seven games against Colombian squads, the first on December 6, 1952, in Ecuador, when Cali won 2-1. Once in Colombia, they lost 2-0 to Santa Fe before 10,000 fans and 4-0 to Millonarios (16,00 fans). Huracán would not lose again. They defeated Quindío, drew with Cali and Boca Juniors, and won their final game against Boca Juniors in Cali.

Rapid Vienna and River Plate played between January and February 1953, in Bogota for a five-team trophy called the *Copa República de Colombia*, which also included Deportivo Cali, Santa Fe, and Millonarios. Beyond this *Copa*, Rapid lost it only additional game, against Boca Juniors in Cali (4-3), with gate receipts of COP 4,000 (USD 1,593).

Data from 14 games of the *Copa* show an average attendance of 22,500. Gate receipts are available for only three games, two of them in Cali. Rapid Vienna's 5-2 debut loss on January 4 had 11,000 fans and COP 27,000 (USD 10,757). The expectations with River Plate were much higher. Nineteen thousand fans witnessed the 3-1 Cali victory, paying COP 49,500 (USD 19,721). The excitement with Millonarios was even larger. On January 18, 1953, 21,000 fans attended the stadium to see Cali's 1-0 victory, paying COP 61,500 (USD 24,502).

Cali went on to win the first four games of the *Copa*, drew the fifth match with Rapid, and lost the second leg game with River Plate 1–4. Santa Fe defeated Rapid in its debut, lost both games against Cali, and lost the first game against River, drawing 3-3 in the second leg. The Austrians did not play the last game against Santa Fe, so the points were awarded to the Bogota team.

Millonarios performed poorly. It lost both games against River Plate and won only three matches, one against each of Rapid, Cali, and Santa Fe. With these results, River Plate, which drew the first game against Rapid but trashed the Austrians 5-0 in the second leg, won the *Copa República de Colombia*. Cali finished second, level on points with Santa Fe.

Two days after Millonarios' defeat against Santa Fe, with just 5,000 in the stands, it faced River Plate again in Caracas, this time thrashing the Argentines 5-1 in the second edition of the *Copa Coronel Marcos Pérez Jiménez*. The lineup was different from the one used in the best days of El Dorado. The

Paraguayan Ramírez had decided to leave at the end of the 1952 season, while the Peruvians Soría and Mosquera moved to the Venezuelan league.

On February 12, 1953, Cozzi, Pini, Zuluaga, Martínez, Rossi, Benegas, Villalba, Villaverde, Di Stéfano, Báez, and Mourín took revenge on River Plate. They would go on to win the tournament, drawing 1-1 in a second match against the Argentine and convincingly beating Rapid Vienna 4-0.

The tournament finished without a second match between Millonarios and Rapid Vienna because the former was already unreachable in the first position. Both, however, decided to play against Venezuelan teams: Rapid against Loyola, and Millonarios against Deportivo Español. Rapid drew with Loyola 3-3, but with a catch: Di Stéfano had played for the Venezuelans as a reinforcement. Millonarios, even without the grand star, won 6-0 against the Venezuelans.

Millonarios, which had had no Christmas break, played and drew 1-1 in its last game in Curaçao on February 22, 1953, before officially ending the friendly season. Di Stéfano had renewed his contract on December 22, 1952, but, as things turned out, that match in Curaçao was the last time he played in the blue jersey of Millonarios. With no records on the goalscorer in that match, his last goal was the opener against Rapid Vienna in Caracas four days earlier.

Millonarios played their first major friendly after the FIFA ban on November 24, 1951, and their last with their top star in Curaçao on February 22, 1953. Over 456 days, with the only break between December 23, 1951, and January 23, 1952, Millonarios played 85 matches in total, 52 of them friendlies, including games against Colombian clubs.

In the calendar year of 1952, the team played 68 games, a number similar to those of top teams in 2025, such as Chelsea, which played 70, Flamengo, around 78, Real Madrid, 72, or PSG, 67. Cali played 58, Santa Fe 54, and Boca Juniors 57. Millonarios' performance rate between November 1951 and February 1953 was 57%.

True, there were still interesting friendlies during the remaining of 1953. In January and February, Cúcuta successfully played ten games in Central America, losing only one. In December 1953, Quindío conducted a similar tour, losing only one of eight matches. In March, Medellín opened its new Atanasio Girardot football stadium with a four-team tournament featuring Atlético Nacional, Alianza Lima, Fluminense (BRA), and Deportivo Cali. Millonarios did a brief two-game tour in Chile and, in November and December, went to Peru, Ecuador, and Central America. By then, the big games were over. There were even European teams visiting, as did Degerfors (SWE), which played five games in Colombia between November and December 1953. However, El Dorado was fading since Di Stéfano left, and by the end of 1953, it was no longer the elite league it had once been.

Overall, the Colombian teams performed well. Figure 2.5 presents the percentage of points won by Colombian clubs over foreign clubs per year of El Dorado. In 1951 and 1952, only Uruguayan teams clearly outperformed the

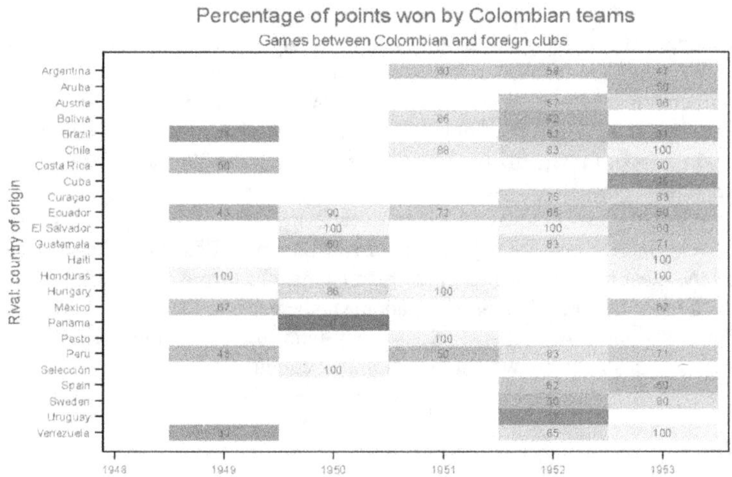


*Figure 2.5* Performance of Colombian teams against foreign clubs

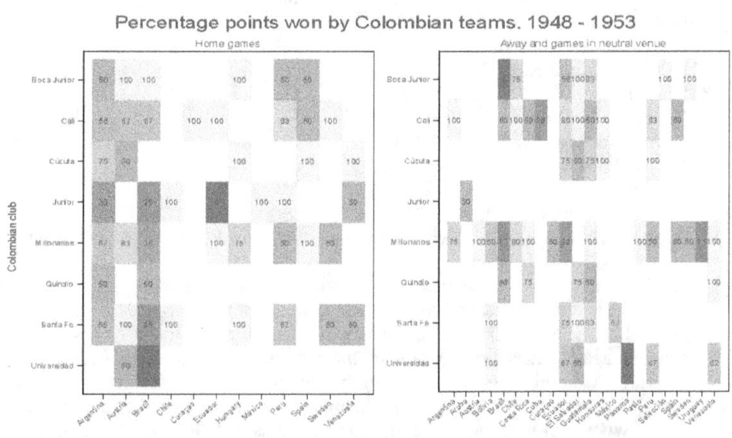


*Figure 2.6* Performance of Colombian clubs: home versus away games

Colombian clubs. The 1953 Cuba figure follows a 7-0 defeat by Deportivo Cali, who had injured players and had to ask their rival for a replacement.[246] In the following game, Cali defeated 2-0 the Spanish Sporting de Gijón, at the time a first-division team. And, of course, there is Brazil. Only in 1952 did Colombian teams manage to outplay them.

It is worth reviewing the results by venue, as traveling was an issue at the time. Millonarios played in 1952 in seven countries, including continental Spain and the Canary Islands. Figure 2.6 reveals, for selected teams, the performance of Colombian clubs against foreign rivals for the period 1948–1953. At home, they outperform most rivals, regardless of country of origin, except for Brazil. The two Cali teams and Quindío can withstand the Brazilians' power.

When reviewing away or neutral-venue matches, Brazil systematically proves superior, as Uruguay did against Millonarios. Ecuadorian teams are, for the most part, inferior to Colombian teams, but surprisingly, Millonarios had a lot of trouble winning in Ecuador. Maybe because they did not take the games seriously, or perhaps because they tend to play in mid-season, they were still unable to show their talents in that country.

## Notes

1. https://fcf.com.co/2012/05/02/https-fcf-com-co-index-php-2012-05-02-la-historia-de-nuestro-futbol/ visited January 12, 2025.
2. See Galvis Ramírez (2008), Ruiz Bonilla (2008) or Worswick (2012).
3. Revista Sábado, October 7, 1950, p. 3.
4. See Galvis Ramírez (2008) or Ruiz Bonilla (2008).
5. El Telegrama, July 21, 1892, p. 8.
6. Santos Molano (2008).
7. El Tiempo, June 28, 1920, p. 7.
8. See Ruíz Bonilla (2008) and Revista Sábado, October 7, 1950, p. 3.
9. Ruíz Bonilla (2008).
10. Revista Sábado, October 7, 1950, p. 3.
11. Revista Sábado, October 7, 1950, p. 3.
12. El Tiempo, March 2, 1938, p. 2.
13. Revista Sábado, October 7, 1950, p. 11.
14. https://www.suin-juriscol.gov.co/viewDocument.asp?id=30040330 visited January 12, 2025.
15. "…the headquarters of the National Associations shall be established every four years by the relevant General Assemblies; however, if the affiliated Leagues demonstrate to the National Commission of Physical Education that their association is acting against the sport they govern, the National Commission may require the Executive Committee to call an assembly, in which a special delegate will represent the Commission, to study the problem and submit the corresponding report." https://www.suin-juriscol.gov.co/viewDocument.asp?id=30040330 visited January 12, 2025.
16. El Tiempo, July 24, 1944, p. 11.
17. El Tiempo, August 14, 1944, p. 11.
18. El Tiempo, February 12, 1945, p. 10.
19. El Tiempo, October 29, 1944, p. 6.
20. El Tiempo, December 11, 1944, p. 1.
21. El Tiempo, February 12, 1945, p. 11.
22. Ruiz Bonilla (2008).
23. Revista Semana, December 4, 1948, p. 10.
24. El Heraldo, June 14, 1948, p. 6.

25 El Tiempo, July 1, 1948, p. 19.
26 El Tiempo, July 6, 1948, p. 2. El Heraldo, July 7, 1948, p. 7.
27 El Heraldo, July 3, 1948, p. 5.
28 El Heraldo, July 7, 1948, p. 7.
29 Goldblatt (2007), p. 277.
30 Wilson (2016), p. 81.
31 Worswick (2012), p. 4.
32 Worswick (2012), p. 4.
33 Diario Gráfico, December 5, 1951, p. 19.
34 Fernández Chavarria (2018), p. 69.
35 Fernández Chavarria (2018), pp. 70–72.
36 Zarama (2023), p. 61.
37 El Heraldo, August 12, 1948, p. 6.
38 El Tiempo, October 8, 1948, p. 11.
39 El Heraldo, September 11, 1948, p. 12.
40 El Heraldo, September 11, 1948, p. 12.
41 El Heraldo, Octobre 16, 1948, p. 7.
42 El Tiempo, October 6, 1948, p. 9.
43 El Heraldo, October 16, 1948, p. 7.
44 El Heraldo, November 13, 1948, p. 7.
45 El Tiempo, January 30, 1949, p. 10.
46 El Tiempo, February 13, 1949, p. 7.
47 El Tiempo, February 24, 1949, p. 19.
48 El Heraldo, February 25, 1949, p. 7.
49 El Heraldo, February 25, 1949, p. 7.
50 El Heraldo, March 2, 1949, p. 7.
51 El Heraldo, February 25, 1949, p. 7.
52 El Tiempo, February 27, 1949, p. 13.
53 El Heraldo, March 5, 1949, p. 11.
54 El Heraldo, March 7, 1949, p. 7.
55 El Heraldo, March 11, 1949, p. 7.
56 El Tiempo, March 11, 1949, p. 7.
57 El Heraldo, May 7, 1949, p. 8.
58 El Heraldo, May 26, 1949, p. 7.
59 El Heraldo, May 28, 1949, p. 7.
60 El Tiempo, October 27, 1949, p. 18.
61 Revista Goles, June 7, 1949, p. 14.
62 Revista El Gráfico, June 17, 1949, p. 55.
63 Borenstein (2023).
64 Revista Goles, May 18, 1948, p. 20.
65 Revista Goles, July 6, 1948, p. 2.
66 Revista Goles, May 18, 1948, p. 20.
67 Revista Goles, July 6, 1948, p. 3.
68 Revista Goles, July 6, 1948, p. 6.
69 Revista Goles, July 6, 1948, p. 5.
70 Revista Goles, July 13, 1948, p. 17.
71 Revista Goles, August 17, 1948, p. 14.
72 Revista Goles, November 9, 1948, p. 2.
73 Revista Goles, November 16, 1948, p. 3.
74 Revista Goles, November 23, 1948, p. 2.
75 Di Stéfano (2000), p. 88.
76 Borenstein (2023), p. 26.
77 Revista River Plate, March 10, 1949, p. 12.

78 Revista Goles, January 11, 1949, p. 16.
79 All revenue data from Argentina is from Colussi, Guris, and Kurhy (n.a.)
80 Di Stéfano (2000).
81 Revista Goles, November 9, 1948, p. 17.
82 Di Stéfano (2000), pp. 85–86.
83 Revista Goles, November 9, 1949, pp. 16–17.
84 The exchange rate in Argentina fluctuated significantly, which accounts for the varying dollar values even when peso amounts remain constant.
85 Revista Goles, February 1, 1949, p. 10.
86 Revista Goles, March 22, 1949, p. 29.
87 Revista River Plate, March 10, 1949, p. 12.
88 Revista Goles, April 4, 1949, p. 7, and Revista River Plate, March 17, 1947, p. 6.
89 Revista River Plate, March 17, 1949, p. 15.
90 Revista Goles, April 4, 1949, p. 7.
91 Revistas Goles, January 11, 1949, pp. 16–17.
92 Revista Goles, April 11, 1949, p. 20.
93 Revista River Plate, April 11, 1949, p. 12.
94 Revista Goles, May 3, 1949, p. 2.
95 Di Stéfano (2000), p. 89.
96 Di Stéfano (2000), p. 93.
97 Revista Goles, May 24, 1949, p. 29.
98 Revista El Gráfico, June 24, 1949, p. 15.
99 Revista Goles, June 14, 1949, p. 11.
100 Alabarces (2018).
101 El Comercio, March 1, 1949, p. 15.
102 La Crónica, May 13, 1949, p. 22.
103 La Crónica, May 7, 1949, p. 22.
104 La Crónica, May 5, 1949, p. 21.
105 La Crónica, May 6, 1949, p. 21.
106 La Crónica, May 13, 1949, p. 22.
107 La Crónica, May 19, 1949, p. 21.
108 La Crónica, May 16, 1949, p. 4.
109 La Crónica, May 17, 1949, p. 21.
110 Bestard (1981).
111 Alabarces (2018).
112 Chamorro (2020), p. 26.
113 Revista Goles, October 26, p. 5.
114 Lorenzo (1970).
115 Potts Harmer (2019), p. 94.
116 Adamson (1996), p. 105.
117 The account of Franklin's move to Colombia is mostly based on Potts Hamer (2019).
118 Potts Harmer (2019), p. 88.
119 Potts Harmer (2019), p. 100.
120 Adamson (1996), p. 104.
121 El Tiempo, June 6, 1950, p. 8; and July 13, 1950, p. 8.
122 The Indian Express, July 3, 1950, p. 7.
123 Potts Harmer (2019), p. 127.
124 Liverpool Echo, August 3, 1950.
125 Potts Harmer (2019), p. 116.
126 Interview with Hernán Peláez (March 17, 2025), where he mentioned having interviewed Mario Abello and saying this.
127 El Heraldo, April 28, p. 7.

128 Wilson (2019).
129 Kowalski and Porter (2012).
130 El Tiempo, November 12, 1950, p. 16.
131 El Heraldo, February 24, 1951, p. 8.
132 https://www.diepresse.com/374537/der-mann-am-zaun visited October 29, 2025.
133 El Tiempo, December 2, 1951, p. 10.
134 Diario Gráfico, June 26, 1952, p. 18.
135 El Tiempo, May 26, 1949, p. 9.
136 La Crónica, May 13, 1949, p. 8.
137 La Crónica, May 20, 1949, p. 9.
138 La Crónica, May 31, 1949, p. 22.
139 Zarama (2023), p. 66.
140 Zarama (2023), p. 66.
141 Ruiz Bonilla (2016), p. 35.
142 Silva (2023), p. 57 and Zarama (2023), p. 67.
143 Revista Goles, August 9, 1949, p. 3.
144 La Crónica, June 8, 1949, p. 4.
145 La Crónica, June 8, 1949, p. 2.
146 Revista Goles, July 5, 1949, p. 11.
147 La Crónica, July 1, 1949, p. 5.
148 Revista Goles, July 12, 1949, p. 10.
149 Revista Goles, July 12, 1949, p. 12.
150 Revista Semana, July 7, 1951, p. 14.
151 Revista Goles, July 5, 1949, p. 28.
152 Revista Goles, July 19, 1949, p. 14. The Torino offer is reported in Silva (2023) p. 63.
153 Revista Goles, July 19, 1949, p. 26.
154 Silva (2023), p. 64.
155 Revista Goles, August 16, 1949, p. 2.
156 River Plate Archive books. Nestor Raúl Rossi.
157 River Plate Archive books. Nestor Raúl Rossi.
158 Revista River Plate, August 11, 1949, No. 254. p. 2.
159 Di Stéfano (2000), p. 94.
160 Revista Goles October 4, 1949, p. 27.
161 Silva (2023), p. 65.
162 Revista Semana, November 17, 1951, p. 34.
163 El Comercio, August 13, 1949. p. 18.
164 Revista Semana, December 17, 1949, p. 28.
165 La Crónica, August 13, 1949, p. 18.
166 El Comercio, August 12, 1949, p. 12.
167 Ruiz Bonilla (2017), p. 18.
168 Soutinho (2015), p. 159.
169 Revista Goles, September 13, 1949, pp. 2–4.
170 Revista Goles, September 13, 1949, p. 2.
171 Revista Goles, September 6, 1949, p. 29.
172 Revista Goles, September 20, 1949, p. 3.
173 Revista Goles, January 3, 1950, pp. 6–7.
174 Loustau tells this story in Revista Goles, January 3, 1959, pp. 2–4.
175 El Tiempo, January 21, 1950, p. 9.
176 Revista Goles, January 17, 1950, p. 29, Revista Goles, January 24, 1950, p. 26, & El Tiempo, January 13, 1950, p. 13.
177 Revista Goles, August 16, 1949, p. 29.
178 El Tiempo, August 12, 1949, p. 18.

179 Revista Goles, January 24, 1950, p. 26.
180 Revista Goles, December 27, 1949, p. 23 and La Opinión (California) December 23, 1949, p. 7.
181 Revista Goles, January 24, 1950, p. 26.
182 Revista Goles, January 17, 1949, pp. 9–11.
183 Revista Goles, January 3, 1950, p. 9, & Revista Goles, March 28, 1949, p. 6.
184 El Tiempo, February 19, 1951, p. 11.
185 El Tiempo, February 2, 1951, p. 9.
186 El Heraldo, March 9, 1950, p. 9.
187 Journal do Brasil, February 12, 1950, p. 7.
188 El Heraldo, September 6, 1950, p. 7.
189 El Heraldo, March 9, 1950, p. 9.
190 El Tiempo, March 27, 1950, p. 13.
191 El Heraldo, April 3, 1950, p. 7.
192 El Tiempo, November 11, 1949, p. 16.
193 Gómez Herrera (2004), p. 32.
194 Gómez Herrera (2004), p. 34.
195 Diario La Opinión, January 3, 1950, p. 7.
196 El Heraldo, January 6, 1950, p. 6.
197 El Tiempo, March 22, 1950, p. 6.
198 Revista Goles, July 18, 1950, p. 21.
199 El Tiempo, March 1, 1951.
200 https://www.inter.it/en/archivio_giocatore/G0685 visited October 8, 2025.
201 Silva Guzmán (2025), pp. 54–55.
202 It is a Cúcuta fan website, but the article is signed by Alfredo Díaz Calderón, a relevant figure in the sporting community of Norte de Santander, and contemporary to that great 1951 team. He probably recalls the figures from the time. https://cucutanuestra.com/temas/libros_nortesantandereanos/historia_del_deporte_de_cucuta/el_futbol_crea_competencia_radial.htm visited October 8, 2025.
203 El Heraldo, June 17, 1950, p. 9.
204 Adamson (1996), p. 105.
205 Potts Harmer (2019), p. 114.
206 The Indian Express, August 21, 1949, p. 7.
207 Edmonton Journal, May 16, 1950, p. 10.
208 El Tiempo, June 6, 1950, p. 10.
209 The Liverpool Football Echo, August 19, 1950.
210 Adamson (1996), pp. 104–107.
211 Archivo Nacional de Colombia, Sección de extranjeros. Sección TD, número 23981.
212 Potts Harmer (2019), p. 114.
213 El Heraldo, September 6, p. 7.
214 Potts Harmer (2019), p. 95.
215 Potts Harmer (2019), p. 153.
216 Adamson (1996), p. 136.
217 El Tiempo, November 29, 1949, p. 16.
218 El Tiempo, February 21, 1950, p. 10.
219 https://semillerosdeportivos.com/los-69-anos-del-campeonato-la-dimayor/ visited October 6, 2025.
220 El Tiempo, March 18, 1950, p. 8.
221 El Tiempo, April 2, 1950, p. 16.
222 La Nación, September 7, 2014, visited October 4, 2025. https://www.nacion.com/puro-deporte/futbol-internacional/futbolistas-tiicos-pasaron-de-una-liga-pirata-al-legalismo-de-hoy/PF52ZBHNNBDEJPDAEMQUTC5644/story/

223 El Tiempo, November 2, 1951, p. 9.
224 Potts Harmer (2019), p. 132.
225 Revista Semana, December 17, 1949, p. 27.
226 El Tiempo, July 4, 1949, p. 13.
227 El Tiempo, August 15, 1949, p. 14.
228 El Tiempo, October 10, 1949, p. 10.
229 El Heraldo, October 11, 1949, p. 11.
230 El Comercio, November 7, 1949, p. 18.
231 El Tiempo, May 23, 1950, p. 8.
232 El Tiempo, November 24, 1950, p. 18.
233 El Tiempo, May 7, 1951, p. 14.
234 Diario Gráfico, December 17, 1951, p. 17.
235 Revista Goles, No. 0184, pp. 20–21.
236 Diario Gráfico, May 21, 1952, p. 18.
237 Di Stéfano (2000), p. 107.
238 Di Stéfano (2000), p. 107.
239 Diario Gráfico, March 14, 1952, p. 17.
240 Diario Gráfico, March 25, 1952, p. 13.
241 Diario Gráfico, March 25, 1952, p. 13.
242 Diario Gráfico, March 25, 1952, p.15.
243 El Tiempo, March 27, 1952, p. 8.
244 Tovar (2014), p. 56.
245 ABC, April 1, 1952, pp. 29–30.
246 El Tiempo, July 13, 1953, p. 16.

## References


ABC. Various numbers. Available at https://www.abc.es/archivo/periodicos/

Adamson, R. (1996). *Bogota Bandit. The Outlaw Life of Charlie Mitten: Manchester United's Penalty King.* Mainstream Publishing Company

Alabarces, P. (2018). *Historia mínima del fútbol en América Latina.* El Colegio de Mexico AC.

Bestard, M. A. (1981). *80 años de fútbol en Paraguay.* Litograf. Asuncion.

Borenstein, A. (2023). *Los Muchachos Futbolistas.* Aguilar Editores. Buenos Aires.

Chamorro, F. (2020). *Revolución de 1947.* Editorial Goya. Asunción.

Colussi, L. A., Guris, C. A., and Kurhy, V. H. (n.a.). *Fútbol Argentino: Crónicas y Estadísticas. Asociación del Fútbol Argentino* [n.p.].

Di Stéfano. A. (2000). *Gracias Vieja.* Aguilar Editores.

Diario Gráfico. Various numbers. Biblioteca Luis Ángel Arango.

Edmonton Journal. Variuous numbers. Available at https://news.google.com/newspapers?nid=gYAb_yFic6IC.

El Comercio. Various numbers. Biblioteca Nacional, and Instituto Riva Agüero, PUCP.

El Heraldo. Various numbers. Archive Diario El Heraldo.

El Telegrama. Various numbers. Biblioteca Nacional.

El Tiempo. Various Numbers. Available at https://news.google.com/newspapers?nid=N2osnxbUuuUC.

Fernández Chavarria, J. L. (2018). El Fútbol en Bogota; Colegios, Origen y Profesionalización de los clubes Santa Fe (1941) y los Millonarios (1946). Master's thesis in history—Universidad de Los Andes. https://repositorio.uniandes.edu.co/server/api/core/bitstreams/09371340-1b51-4db7-b887-9bca14bd2664/content.

Galvis Ramírez, A. (2008). *100 años de fútbol en Colombia*. Editorial Planeta Colombia S.A.

Goldblatt, D. (2007). *The Ball Is Round: A Global History of Football*. Penguin UK.

Gómez Herrea, D. (2004). 60 años de historia. *Gol del Pereira*. Fondo Editorial de Risaralda.

Journal do Brasil. Various numbers. Available at https://www.jb.com.br/acervo.

Kowalski, R., and Porter, D. (2012). Cold War football: British–European encounters in the 1940s and 1950s. In Stephen Wagg and David L. Andrews (eds.) *East Plays West: Sport and the Cold War* (pp. 64–81). Routledge.

La Crónica. Various numbers. Biblioteca Nacional.

La Opinión. Various numbers. Available at https://news.google.com/newspapers?nid=A8NefVh_EAoC

Liverpool Echo. Various numbers. Available at https://britishnewspaperarchive.co.uk/.

Lorenzo, C. (1970). *100 años de fútbol. Historia del fútbol uruguayo*. "Los Emigrantes". No 20.

Nadel, J. H. (2014). *Fútbol!: Why Soccer Matters in Latin America*. University Press of Florida.

Potts Harmer, A. (2019). *England's Greatest Defender. The Untold Story of Neil Franklin*. Red Door.

Revista El Gráfico. Various numbers. Biblioteca Nacional.

Revista Goles. Various Numbers.

Revista River Plate. Various Numbers. Club Atlético River Plate Archive.

Revista Sábado, Various Numbers. Available at Biblioteca Luis Ángel Arango.

Revista Semana. Various numbers. Biblioteca Nacional Bogota.

Ruiz Bonilla, G. (2008). *La Gran Historia del Fútbol Profesional Colombiano*. Ediciones Dayscript.

Ruiz Bonilla, G. (2016). *Millonarios FC. 70 años*. Mundo Fútbol.

Ruiz Bonilla, G. (2017). *Medellín, el Poderoso de la Montaña*. Mundo Fútbol.

Santos Molano, E. (2005). Fútbol, una pasión incontenible in *Revista Credencial No 185*.

Silva Guzmán, M. (2023). *El Mejor Equipo del Mundo. La Increíble y Romántica Historia del "Ballet Azul" (Millonarios 1949–1953)*. Planeta.

Soutinho, Felipe (2015). *San Pontoni del Papa. Vida y goles de un bendito del fútbol*. Felipe Soutinho.

The Indian Express. Various Numbers. Available at https://news.google.com/newspapers?nid=P9oYG7HA76QC.

Tovar, J. (2014). *Números redondos*. Grijalbo.

Wilson, J. (2019). *The Names Heard Long Ago: How the Golden Age of Hungarian Soccer Shaped the Modern Game*. Bold Type Books.

Worswick, C. (2012). The Ball and the Gun in *The Blizzard Football Quarterly* No 7, January.

Zarama, J. G. (2023). Yo puse a bailar al ballet azul. Biografía de Alfonso Senior Quevedo. Amazon Ed.

# 3 The fall of El Dorado

## Exodus, punishment, and agreements

Captivating players from around the world with promises of riches beyond their dreams, the country, in the eyes of the institutionalized football world, was not El Dorado but pirates stealing their valuable assets. Not surprisingly, pressure mounted from England to Argentina to stop the flow of players. The initial reaction in each league was very similar: punish the player by barring them from playing in the league again. Due to FIFA rulings, sanctioned players could not play in any other affiliated league. Argentine Football Association (AFA) had passed a resolution to expel those players who refused to sign a contract. Thus, willingly or not, players like Rossi and Di Stéfano were forced to sign a contract with River Plate. However, claiming that, before signing the new contract, the club owed them their Christmas bonus, among others, they unilaterally terminated the contract and flew to Colombia.

As others traveled North, AFA took drastic measures to stop the migration. As early as August 1949, following complaints by Huracán and Platense, AFA expelled Adolfo Pedernera, Manuel Giudice, and Oscar Corzo. Stronger measures were implemented months later. In October, AFA voted to ban for life anyone leaving for an unaffiliated league from playing in any Argentine club, adding that amnesty could only be granted when all AFA members voted unanimously.

The severity of AFA's resolution had two consequences. First, the clubs implicitly accepted losing their assets. Second, the players who had left, even if interested in returning, had no option but to stay in Colombia.

Argentina implemented every tactic in the playbook to stop the exodus. In February 1950, the government issued a decree stating that no Argentine citizen could leave the country if they had pending accounts with the Tax Office. As the club issued the clearance certificate, the measure was initially taken as the perfect way to stop players. Indeed, Vicente de la Mata and Arnaldo were the first to taste the effect of the decree. While at the airport, ready to fly to Bogota, lacking the paperwork, they were not allowed to leave the country.

DOI: 10.4324/9781003396024-3

The notification caught two other players, Camilo Cervino and Oscar Sastre, in Chile on their way to Deportivo Cali. Stuck in Chile for a couple of days, they eventually received all the paperwork and continued the route to Colombia. Although "Capote" de la Mata ended up signing for Independiente (ARG), Arnaldo did fly to Colombia just a few weeks after his first attempt. In practice, the measure had little effect.

In April, San Lorenzo formally accused the players' union of failing to condemn breaches of contract by its members and initiated legal action against its former players: Perucca, Pontoni, Benegas, "Pibe" Rial, and the Colombian Efraín "el Caimán" Sánchez. Still, the exodus continued.

Overall, with the sanctions in place, even players who had left without a contract, like Pedernera, remained vanished. Moreover, even when retired, or as Pedernera in 1952, in the process of retiring, they were not allowed to serve as managers in the Argentine league. Indeed, in June 1952, Pedernera, back in Argentina, was "advisor" to the managerial staff at *Ferro Carril Oeste*, awaiting appointment as full-time coach of the first squad. Meanwhile, with no decision in Pedernera's favor, the club supported his trip back to Millonarios to play in an international friendly tour. Of course, the one hundred dollars a day offered by the Colombians strongly motivated the *Maestro*. Months passed, and by 1953, Pedernera left his country again because AFA still refused to give him the required amnesty to work at home. Again, he joined Millonarios while on tour, this time in Chile.

Sanctions were the standard token everywhere. Neil Franklin, who lasted only two months in Bogota, was the first Englishman to return, and the FA used him as an example of the consequences. The story of Franklin's escape is a novel in itself, although he was not the only English player who left without finishing his contract. Robert Flawell, under contract until 1952, waited until he was paid all 1950 season bonuses and salaries, then left unannounced on December 12, 1950.[1]

Returning to Franklin's story, some points seem uncontroversial. His wife was pregnant and worried about the baby's British citizenship if he were born in Colombia, so the couple decided to play it safe and fly back to England. According to Franklin, Santa Fe authorized him to fly with his wife to New York.[2] The plan was to see his wife off to London, returning then to Bogota. In New York, Franklin claimed that there was no reservation for his wife on the flight to London. Stranded in New York, he called Robledo, Santa Fe's President, to inform him that he would not fly back to Bogota until his wife was safely on her way to London. Despite Robledo's plea to return on time for the next match, he stayed in New York, promising to return promptly.

At this point, Evelyn Webster, a reporter for the Daily Express, appears in the story. According to Franklin, she pitied them and hosted the family in her apartment. Eventually, the entire family managed to fly back to London. Franklin claimed that he had left all his clothes in Bogota and that, even while flying back home, he planned to return. Robledo, however, was offended because he had to face the press and explain why the English star would not be playing for Santa Fe. Robledo claimed that Evelyn Webster induced Franklin to escape, paying his family's tickets in exchange for the exclusive on his story in the Daily Express.[3]

Franklin's plans will probably remain unknown. Upon arrival in England, he kept in touch with Santa Fe, and it seems that he was considering returning to Bogota.[4] Eventually, however, he decided staying in England would be in his best interest. Stanley Matthews claims in his autobiography that Neil only received one week's wages, probably no more than £60.[5] This would support Robledo's theory that Franklin sold the exclusive to the Daily Express in exchange for the return tickets for his family. However, as noted earlier, Colombian clubs used to pay substantial sums in advance to attract foreign players.

Either way, Santa Fe sued Franklin in England, demanding the three thousand five hundred dollars they claimed they had paid him upon signing the contract, his air ticket from London to Bogota, and the round-trip tickets for his wife and child. Additionally, they sought reimbursement for the expenses incurred in finding Franklin a house in Bogota, the cost of furniture and the hotel expenses. Matthews' theory holds thin.

When leaving England, Franklin's suspension remained "effective until the players apply to this Association for, and granted reinstatement".[6] He had gone in May 1950, and by September of that year, he was applying to the FA for reinstatement.

The FA did not remove Franklin's suspension until January 31, 1951. Meanwhile, he would remain a retained player of Stoke City FC without receiving any income. But Stoke had no interest in Franklin. The situation, to modern eyes, was unacceptable: Franklin was not under contract, was not allowed to train, and was not receiving any income, yet the club was negotiating to sell him. Franklin moved to Hull City, which was then in the second division. He would never again play in England's top tier.

Franklin's fate is an example of players chasing the riches of *El Dorado*. Before the 1950–1951 season, Mitten had not signed his new contract with Manchester United. Yet, under the retain-and-transfer system, the club expected him to sign. Instead, Mitten arrived at Bogota's airport on July 8, 1950. He flew back to England on July 22, 1951. [7]

At some point in his biography, Mitten suggests that he had the chance to move from Colombia to Real Madrid.[8] He mentions that Madrid's President, Santiago Bernabéu, told him to move because he was trying to "get the best players in the world". Truth or not, he decided to return to England. In half an hour, the FA disciplinary court banned him for six months and fined him £250 (USD 700), the equivalent of six months' salary.[9] On top of that, Manchester United also fined him £250, paid no wages, and transferred him to Fulham for £22,000 (USD 61,600), despite Mitten's attempts to convince boss Matt Busby to let him play with his old team.[10] Irony, Manchester United won the 1951–1952 First Division, while Fulham finished last. Like Franklin, Mitten would never again play in England's top-tier division.

Peru, where the exodus originated in the lack of professionalism (and, for some elite players, in disciplinary sanctions following the *Las Palmas* events), proved to be the key to the beginning of the end of *El Dorado*. By mid-1950, a football player in Peru was either "amateur" or "not amateur", a veiled way of covering up professionalism.[11] Peru, whose football was highly regarded across the subcontinent, had already been South American champions twice, in 1935 and 1939. In the 1949 championship celebrated in Brazil, they finished third behind the home team and Paraguay.

Following the *Las Palmas* events, six players, including superstar Valeriano López, were sanctioned for life, leaving them few options when deciding whether to move to Colombia. Moreover, given the absence of professional football in Peru, clubs there initially authorized their players to travel to Colombia. However, with nearly 50 Peruvian players flying to Colombia between 1949 and 1951, sanctions were imposed, banning some for life and preventing them from playing friendlies in Lima.

It all changed with the 50th anniversary of Alianza Lima, one of the most popular Peruvian football clubs, in February 1951. Ahead of the official celebrations, Alianza's President, General José Vásquez Benavides addressed a letter to the country's President, General Manuel A. Odría asking the government

> for the sake of progress in our most popular sport, currently in such dramatic decline, and for the broad satisfaction of all fans in the Republic, please grant, through the corresponding sporting authorities, a general amnesty for all banned national players.[12]

The President replied swiftly while granting Alianza Lima the grounds for their stadium:

> As proof of my desire, which is also that of all sports lovers, I have arranged for a general amnesty that lifts the punishments imposed on our football players, opening the doors so that those who sincerely love the Homeland may once again put their capability and effort at its service, to offer new and more resounding victories.[13]

Initially, the National Sports Committee, the government's sporting agency, "recommended" that the Peruvian Football Federation declare a 90-day general amnesty.[14] This spurred a national debate because the clubs understood that the President was issuing an order and that it was not in the spirit of his declaration to delay the amnesty. Eventually, the amnesty became effective as other clubs began to address more pressing issues, including how to pay the returning players.

The press and the clubs began a campaign to bring back the lost stars. Having broken his ankle in June 1950, Valeriano López was not in the best shape for the early games of 1951. Peruvians argued he was mistreated by Cali officials, who were working to find him a substitute. Indeed, the Peruvian coach, Magallanes, had left the team and was replaced by the Argentine Carlos Peucelle. By 1951, Cali was no longer a "Peruvian team" and imported the Argentine Norberto Payroux for the new season.[15]

The players played their roles in the story. Valeriano López wrote an open letter:

> I send my warmest congratulations to the President of the Republic, to the members of the Federation, and to you, Mr. Director, for lifting the punishments that weighed on us. I feel happier than ever at the prospect of playing on my home turf and putting on great shows as a professional. I hope to return as soon as possible to demonstrate what I have learned in football to all the fans.[16]

Thus, bringing back the Peruvian players from Colombia was legal, but how could a nonprofessional league convince them to leave *El Dorado*? Around February 1951, the clubs proposed an international friendly season in Lima to raise funds to pay the returning players an amount equivalent to what they earned in Colombia. However, to make the season profitable, which eventually brought America from Brazil for USD 3,500 per game, the clubs asked the government for tax cuts, which took effect in October when the government reduced the 35% tax on gross income to 5%.[17] In March, with professionalism finally part of the landscape, the clubs drew up a standard contract which an emissary brought to Colombia to lure the Peruvian stars. Given the expected costs of repatriation, they created a recruitment fund whose initial allocation (including the tax cuts) came from the revenues from America's visit to Peru and a "lightning" friendly tournament that Tabaco won over Alianza Lima.[18]

Eventually, by the end of October, the fund had 445,873.24 soles (USD 29,216), 294,000 (USD 19,266) produced by international friendlies in Lima, 33,026 (USD 2,164) from friendlies played by the Peruvian National team, and the rest provided either directly by the Peruvian Football Federation or by some government agency.[19] A decent amount of money, but still far from the figures that Colombian clubs were dealing with at the time.

Meanwhile, Alianza Lima executive Benjamín Cisneros traveled to La Paz to negotiate the return of Ismael Soria, an undisputed starter for Millonarios. Alianza could negotiate with Soria because he left for Colombia without ever playing in the Peruvian first division. However, to avoid competition, the clubs decided that the players should return to their clubs of origin.

To increase the pressure, the clubs sent an emissary to Colombia to convince the Peruvian players that returning home was an option. The situation grew tighter for Colombian clubs as rumors surfaced that several players had tried to leave the country in breach of their contracts. Indeed, in mid-March 1951, Valeriano López (Deportivo Cali) and Juan Lecca, Luis Portanova, and Ernesto Morales, all from Once Deportivo, the rumor said, were caught attempting to secure passports to abandon the country and return to Peru.[20] Days later, the Once Deportivo players and the club stated that the accusations were false. In their letter, they noted that the plan was to return to Peru upon completion of their contracts.[21]

A month later, Valeriano López wrote a letter to Deportivo Cali's President, Carlos Sarmiento, asking him to free him from his contract set to expire in August 1951 because he had not wholly recovered from his ankle injury, leaving him with an inadequate playing level. López arrived in Lima on April 24, 1951, using the airplane ticket and the USD 500—all that he had requested from Sport Boys.[22] Under his new contract, he received a signing bonus of 20,000 soles (USD 1,344), 15,000 soles (USD 1,008) provided by the recruitment fund, plus a monthly wage of 1,000 soles (USD 67) and winning bonuses. Figures significantly lower than those offered by the Colombian clubs at the time.

Eighteen Peruvian players had returned by mid-May, leaving 28 still in Colombia. Led by Valeriano López, other cracks, like Tito Drago, "Vides" Mosquera, Juan Lecca, "Titina" Castillo, and Luis Navarrete, left *El Dorado* thanks to the presidential amnesty.

## The Lima Pact: taming the pirate league

A deal was unlikely as long as the Dimayor league remained profitable. If clubs and players made money, if fans enjoyed high-quality football, there was no sporting or financial reason to back down. However, there were pressing issues. On the one hand, the league was in financial distress, with some clubs struggling to meet their obligations. On the other hand, Colombian clubs' ability to play abroad or host foreign teams was limited because FIFA would not authorize such games, thereby limiting revenue sources. Thus, pressure over Colombia kept piling up.

The Colombian matter was of utmost importance to FIFA and was on the agenda of the XIV FIFA Congress held in Rio de Janeiro during the World Cup. The debate began on June 23, 1950, but first, Colombia had to solve its domestic problems. Thus, the Colombian Football Association sent Eduardo de Castro to Brazil, while Efraín Borrero and Mario Márquez—the president and treasurer of Adefútbol, respectively—flew to Bogota to negotiate a truce with Dimayor.

On June 20, positive news emerged. With the strongest Dimayor men present, including Mario Abello (Junior), Humberto Salcedo Fernández (Universidad), Carlos Sarmiento (Deportivo Cali), and Alfonso Senior (Millonarios), the accord stated, among other topics, that Dimayor would not bring more players without the FIFA transfer and that it would pay Adefútbol 1% of the gross revenues of each match. On their part, Adefútbol would reaffiliate Dimayor and amend its statutes.[23]

In Brazil, de Castro announced that the division was a matter of the past and that the country would create a new unified Football Association that would pay for every player who had arrived without the required permit. Argentina still voted against that proposal because it was unclear that the players would return home immediately.[24]

While de Castro was in Brazil announcing the unification of Colombian football, divisions were rising back home. Dimayor had selected its statutory auditor, Jorge Garcés, to travel to Brazil to attend the FIFA Congress. To travel, he requested that Adefútbol issue the respective credentials. Dimayor understood that Mr. Garcés would represent Colombia as an observer and that Eduardo de Castro would have the right to vote. However, when Garcés arrived at the office of the President of Adefútbol to request the credentials, he was denied. Reunification started on the wrong foot.

Days later, Adefútbol decided to recognize, not reaffiliate, Dimayor. According to Adefútbol, reaffiliating would legalize Dimayor's actions. After extensive sessions, in August, Adefútbol and Dimayor agreed on the statutes and the composition of the Board: three members for Dimayor and two for Adefútbol. The latter, however, would control the two most important positions, President and Treasurer. Regarding the imports of new players, however, nothing changed. In practice, Dimayor and Adefútbol kept operating independently, and the accord was not enforced.

Indeed, while Argentina kept seeking compensation, players kept coming to Colombia. For instance, in October 1950, AFA sent an emissary, Enrique Eduardo Pinto, to negotiate with the Football Federation for a compensation package. According to his calculations, Colombian clubs owed COP 2.000.000 (USD 1,020,408). Upon an agreement, first-division Argentine clubs could play in Colombia.[25] According to Pinto, the Colombians never offered more than a symbolic payment.[26] The conditions were unacceptable for Dimayor, and his trip was seen in Colombia more as an act of arrogance than conciliation.

Later that year, after the domestic tournament finished, Dimayor clubs requested Adefútbol's permission to tour Central America, Guatemala in particular. Adefútbol denied the permits, keeping instead communication channels open with foreign football authorities to restrict Colombian teams from playing abroad and foreigners from visiting Colombia. Despite the lack of permits, both Cali and Boca Juniors flew to tour Guatemala and El Salvador, while Huracán visited Panama. The Guatemalan Football Association, it is worth noting, thanked the visit of Cali and Boca Juniors and explicitly said that "the games were played without any obstacles since Guatemala has no relationship with FIFA".[27]

The division between Adefútbol and Dimayor was such that, in February 1951, Adefútbol announced that Colombia would not organize the South American Championship of Nations because the division between amateur and professional entities made it impossible.

For AFA, things were getting worse. In November 1950, news spread across Colombia that the Ecuadorian Football Federation would leave FIFA and join Dimayor. Some of their top teams, including Barcelona and Emelec, apparently decided to move, and there were also some mentions that Venezuela would join Dimayor.[28] It was Bolívar's dream, turned into football: the *Gran Colombia* Football Division. But it was just a dream; the idea never took off.

For FIFA, solving the Colombian problem had become a priority. The threat of dissent from several professional leagues and the possibility that others might follow the example of the pirate league could jeopardize the institution's global power. While Dimayor dreamt of spreading the revolution, FIFA's executive committee, in December 1950, assigned Luis Valenzuela (Chilean President of CONMEBOL), Ottorino Barassi (Italy and honorary FIFA Secretary), and Luis Aranha (Brazil and FIFA vice president) to prepare a report on the Colombian problem for the meetings that would take place in March 1951 in Madrid (Spain).[29] Valenzuela and Barassi traveled to Colombia in preparation for the Congress, where they met separately with the representatives of Adefútbol and Dimayor. Upon leaving the country on their way to Madrid, Valenzuela and Barassi mentioned having reached a basis for an agreement but made no specifics.

Weeks later, upon returning to Chile, Valenzuela clarified that FIFA had suggested creating a new association in which Adefútbol would control amateur football, Dimayor would oversee professional football, and together they would handle international matters.[30] At the time, however, there were no specifics about any agreement principles, and the fuzziness around communicating any deal became apparent just weeks later.

Between March 31 and April 2, 1951, in Madrid, FIFA discussed the Colombian problem. The final statement announced a potential solution with a preliminary accord between the parties.[31] In the press conference, Jules Rimet, FIFA's President declarations, altered the balance behind the negotiations held in Colombia by Valenzuela and Barassi with Dimayor. His April 4 statement, saying that an accord to disqualify for life the players who went to Colombia was the "simplest" solution, sparked strong reactions. He added that FIFA kept communication channels open with the legal Colombian Football Association and did little to avoid what came later.[32] Rimet's statement surprised Colombia because Valenzuela and Barassi had left days earlier, with the word sanction absent from their vocabulary. Indeed, almost immediately, Dimayor released a statement informing that they had received no official communication from FIFA.[33]

Moreover, Russo, AFA's representative in Madrid, announced details of the agreement that, apparently, Dimayor and FIFA had reached. His words ignited a debate. In Argentina, some celebrated because they initially understood that Dimayor had agreed to stop hiring foreign players without the transfer papers. However, Valenzuela and Barassi's basic agreement with Dimayor, beyond banning further illegal imports, proposed some compensation in exchange for allowing all players to remain in Colombia. Despite the news of a deal, Argentine players continued to flee. Thus, seeking explanations, the Argentine press informed that for Colombia, the agreement meant they could still hire players with whom they were already negotiating. Further news dispatches, as players kept flying, informed that Colombians could keep seeking football players in Argentina until the accord came into effect. [34]

In Colombia, meanwhile, Camilo Guzmán Cabal, Dimayor's general manager, declared that a basic agreement existed between Dimayor and FIFA but required the dissolution of Adefútbol. The amateur football association saw its position in FIFA and Colombia at risk. Just days after the FIFA Congress, they released an official, open letter to the two Barranquilla teams, Junior and Sporting, demanding that they take a position because Dimayor was on the verge of moving the headquarters to Bogota. Adefútbol expected Junior and Sporting to leave Dimayor under such circumstances. [35] Their concerns were beyond football; they were about regional pride, survival, and subnational power imbalances.

At this point, it was clear that solving the problem required two prerequisites. First, two interlocutors were too many. Adefútbol and Dimayor had to solve their domestic differences. Second, the Colombian clubs would not pay fines or compensation for the players they brought. For Dimayor, finding a solution was also critical - their FIFA membership meant Colombian teams could compete internationally and host prominent foreign clubs. This international engagement represented a vital pathway for addressing the financial difficulties plaguing many clubs.

Things were aligning, but required a nudge. In August 1951, several South American football associations, including Paraguay, Ecuador, Argentina, and, of course, Adefútbol, wrote separate letters to the Colombian President, Laureano Gomez, asking him to intervene to unify Colombian football.[36]

During a Cali meeting that ended on August 20, Dimayor agreed to create a high-level commission, including Bogota's mayor, to study the steps to resolve the situation with FIFA.[37] Days later, Aranha and Valenzuela, in

Bogota, discussed with Adefútbol its concerns about who should serve as President of the unified association and the location of the headquarters. With Dimayor, the FIFA officers understood that its primary concern was to deal with its players. The FIFA emissaries departed with the groundwork laid for resolving Colombian football's internal division. On the one hand, aside from the impossibility of paying any compensation, it was clear that foreign players would have to remain in Colombia under some figure to be determined. Conversely, Adefútbol and Dimayor needed to work out how to function under a unified structure.

Despite Colombian government officials showing limited interest in domestic football, they even sought a friendly settlement. Government and Dimayor representatives flew to Barranquilla on August 10, 1951. With representatives from the Ministry of Education and the Foreign Office, as well as Humberto Pérez Restrepo, Manuel Correa Valencia, and Alfonso Senior from Dimayor, it would be a definitive meeting.

The agreement stated that the Board of the Colombian Football Association would have two members from Adefútbol, two from Dimayor, and a fifth member, the Ministry of Education, which would act as President. While Dimayor agreed to accept Adefútbol's and FIFA's norms, Adefútbol accepted Dimayor as an organization with full rights. The entry and exit of foreign FIFA-affiliated teams would be on standby pending international settlement. Lastly, Adefútbol's headquarters would remain in Barranquilla.[38]

This time, the deal was enforced. Following the announcement, Junior requested Dimayor to register "a Hungarian player, José Fabián, who was living in Italy".[39] It most likely refers to Iosif Fabian, a Romanian player at the time playing in Bari. The demand was denied in a clear sign that the deal would hold this time. Adefútbol, on their part, called the amateur leagues to debate the agreement with Dimayor. The deal, which required professional clubs to pay 4% of gross revenues to the amateur leagues and 1% to Adefútbol, was approved in Barranquilla on October 12, 1951.[40]

The final steps took place in Lima during the October 1951 Extraordinary Football Congress. The objective of the Congress was to ratify Lima as the host of the 1952 South American Football Championship. Delegates from all of South America were present in Lima, which allowed Luis Valenzuela to bring the Colombian situation to the table. The Colombian delegates, Efraín Borrero and Jorge Garcés, arrived in Lima on October 20. Having Dimayor agreed to recognize the Colombian Football Association as the country's leading football organization, there was an optimistic outlook for what the meetings would yield.

To resolve the situation, there were initially three alternatives on the table. The Peruvian delegation asked for compensation to the clubs affected by the "pirate football", 20.000 soles (USD 1,310) per player, and demanded the return of its players.[41] It was an unacceptable alternative for Colombia because the compensation amounts required were well beyond the club's financial capacity. Argentina proposed a more realistic alternative. They asked for no compensation, but Colombia should pay for the damage to the clubs through tours. The idea of sending Argentine clubs to Colombia and charging enough to pay for the players lost to Dimayor had been around since 1949.[42] Adding to the Argentine suggestion, the Uruguayans proposed that the Colombian clubs could keep the players for up to three years.

The negotiations were complex, but at 3 a.m. on October 24, 1951, an agreement was reached. The resulting statement, issued by CONMEBOL, is known in history as the "Lima Pact".[43] The main point of the agreement was that all players currently in Colombian clubs could remain until October 15, 1954. On October 16, they would be reinstated to their original associations. Beyond the return of the players, neither Argentina, Brazil, nor Uruguay requested any compensation, asking only about the possibility of making tours to Colombia. It was simultaneously a diplomatic triumph for Colombian negotiators and the beginning of the end of a unique experiment in world football.

Peru agreed to sign the final statement in exchange for the return of three players who had left without authorization and for a tour to Lima by two of the top five Colombian teams, which would charge only 25% of the gate receipts, net of taxes. The Peruvian Football Federation would pay for the round-trip tickets and accommodation. The three players were Rigoberto Felandro, Félix Castillo, and Eliseo Morales, who had to return upon completion of their contracts. Finally, the Peruvians ensured that Juan Lecca, who had returned to Peru with the amnesty but was negotiating with a Colombian club, would not be allowed to play in Colombia.[44]

Paraguay settled for a minimum of seven games played by the Paraguayan national team in Colombia, charging USD 3,000 per game, plus an additional USD 500 for a draw or USD 1,500 if they won.[45] It never happened.

Following Peru and the Lima Pact, Brazil, Chile, Paraguay, and Uruguay declared an amnesty to their players. On the contrary, Argentina kept the debate over whether they should declare an amnesty ongoing until April 1954. Still, in March 1953, AFA denied amnesty to around 50 players who Colombian clubs had released. Names such as René Pontoni, Mario Fernández, or Antonio Báez could play anywhere, under the conditions stated in the Lima Pact, except in their homeland.[46]

By April 1954, it was an almost unanimous cry for amnesty in Argentina. By the end of April, the Argentine Sports Confederation and the Olympic Committee granted full amnesty to every Argentine athlete. AFA, which still required a unanimous vote, had to ratify the amnesty.[47] It did so, marking the end of *El Dorado*. Still, in a bold twist, approaching the October 1954 deadline, Colombia asked AFA to postpone the deadline. The answer was a hard no.

**The full text of the Lima Pact is as follows:**

***FIRST*** *- Express the satisfaction for the recent unification of Colombian football, based on Dimayor's reincorporation into the Colombian Football Association, whereby, henceforth, any disputes would be resolved within the orbit of FIFA.*

***SECOND*** *- The delegations' members of this Congress, with the authority to do so, declare that they authorize all players belonging to them who currently play in Colombian clubs to continue doing so until October 15, 1954, inclusive, in matches that take place within or outside that country.*

***THIRD*** *- The players referred to in this resolution will be automatically reinstated to their associations of origin starting October 16, 1954.*

***FOURTH*** *- Within thirty days from today, the Colombian Football Association commits and is obligated to send to all associations affiliated with the South American Football Confederation and to its committee, the complete list of players registered and active as of October 15, 1951, for the purposes provided in point two.*

***FIFTH*** *- The Colombian Football Association may not transfer to any foreign association any players whose situation is contemplated in point two, except by mutual agreement with the Association of the player's country of origin.*

***SIXTH*** *- The Colombian Football Association reserves the right to authorize any of the referred players to return to their Association of origin before the expiration of the mentioned deadline - October 15, 1954.*

***SEVENTH*** *- Any doubt or dispute that may arise in the fulfillment or interpretation of this agreement, as well as regarding the situation of the players subject to it, or unforeseen cases, will be resolved by the South American Football Confederation, for which purpose the affiliated associations designate it as the sole arbitrator, whose decision will be final and without any recourse.*

***EIGHTH*** *- A copy of this resolution shall be sent to FIFA for all its effects.*

***NINTH*** *- For this resolution to be fully authorized, it shall be signed by the delegates attending the session.*

## *Financial realities*

The players' salaries were to be supported mainly by two revenue streams: attendance and friendlies' fees. In practice, however, attendance proved insufficient, forcing many clubs to plead for support from benefactors, local or regional governments, and the community. Even before the Lima Accord, many teams struggled to comply with its foreign superstars.

The summary of El Dorado's cycle is illustrated by the number of teams that competed in Dimayor's league between 1948 and 1954. The 1948 league featured ten teams from five cities: Bogota (Millonarios, Santa Fe, Universidad), Medellin (Atlético Municipal, Independiente Medellin), Cali (Deportivo

Cali, América), Barranquilla (Junior), and Manizales (Once Deportivo, Deportes Caldas). Regulatory norms allowed only two teams per city. Thus, the third Bogota team, Universidad, was forced to play in Pereira. Worth noting that it was a closed league with no relegation or promotion.

The first tournament, with foreigners but no superstars, was a success. For the 1949 season, five additional teams joined the league: Boca Juniors (Cali), Atlético Bucaramanga, Huracán (Medellin), Deportivo Barranquilla, and Deportivo Pereira. Dimayor abolished the rule that restricted a third team in a city and, for reasons already presented, expelled Junior. Thus, Universidad moved back to Bogota, and played on Saturdays as did Boca Juniors in Cali.

The league continued to grow in 1950, now with 16 teams. Junior came back, and a new team from a new city joined the professional tournament: Cúcuta Deportivo. In Barranquilla, Sporting replaced Deportivo Barranquilla. In 1951, two additional clubs joined: Deportes Quindío (Armenia) and Deportivo Samarios (Santa Marta). Atlético Municipal changed its name to the one it is known for today: Atlético Nacional.

Manizales was too small to have two teams; thus, for the 1952 league, they merged into Deportivo Manizales. Huracán and Independiente Medellín retired, leaving Medellin with only Atlético Nacional. The league continued to shrink in 1953, with just 12 teams competing. América, Deportivo Manizales, and Universidad disappeared.

Unión Magdalena replaced Deportivo Samarios in Santa Marta. América and Independiente Medellín reappeared in 1954, but Atlético Bucaramanga, Cúcuta Deportivo, Deportivo Pereira, Sporting, and Junior did not participate. In Manizales, a team was born: Atlético Manizales. Figure 3.1 depicts the inverse U-shaped evolution of the number of participants, starting and returning to ten with El Dorado's heydays in 1951.

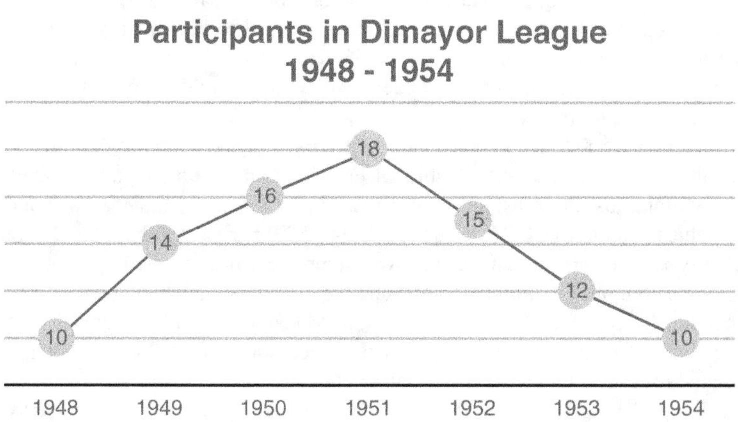


*Figure 3.1* Active clubs in the league, 1948–1954

Initially, the clubs operated as corporations regulated by the government's Superintendency of Corporations, meaning that, like any other firm, they had to balance their books. However, partly to address the financial difficulties and partly to avoid directly aiding the clubs, the national government suggested in September 1952 that the clubs become Sporting Societies, a process that was only enforced by 1953.

The primary revenue source, naturally, stems from match attendance. The numbers, presented elsewhere, suggest that they were insufficient to fund the club's operations. Friendly games, particularly with foreign teams, both at home and abroad, were another significant source, not only because of attendance but also because of the fee typically received when traveling abroad. Consequently, international seasons became significantly more important after the Lima Accord. However, they posed a financial risk because foreign teams usually traveled to Colombia for a fee, with all expenses paid. As a result, insufficient attendance led to the clubs' investments turning into losses.

Attendance revenues are derived from both home games and away matches, the latter through a revenue-sharing system. In 1950, for a revenue stream of up to COP 5,000 (USD 2,550), the away team would receive up to COP 1,000 (USD 510). Gate receipts between COP 5,000 and COP 15,000 (USD 7,650) had the away team receiving 30% of gross revenues; for values over COP 15,000, 15%.[48] By 1952, the scheme was simpler. Each team received COP 1,500 for away games.

Other revenues came from member fees, as some teams operated like clubs, offering amenities in exchange for membership. As many clubs struggled to survive, they resorted to unconventional sources, mostly local or regional government funding, benefactors' capital injections, and, in some cases, the community. On the cost side, clubs had to pay all players' expenses (including salaries, bonuses, agreed plane tickets, among others), fees to Dimayor and Adefútbol, stadium rentals, and other items related to health care or public services. An essential item was the payments to Dimayor, because if they were not up to date at the beginning of each league, they would be excluded from the upcoming tournament.

There are a few detailed accounts of teams' balance sheets at the time. A notable exception reported in Table 3.1 presents four-year aggregate accounts for Millonarios, the most successful team in El Dorado. Matchday average revenues amount to COP 861,631 (USD 343,279) per year, although they are clearly not uniformly distributed. Two items are worth extracting from the revenue column. First, note that Millonarios had some merchandising-related income. It represented just 0,16% of total revenues, but it is suggestive of the club's standards. Second, member fees accounted for 54.5% of nongame-related revenues, totaling 2% of total revenue.

Table 3.1 also shows the expenses, including all items previously described. Note that stadium rental is a non-negligible 6.5% of total costs, that payments to Dimayor and Adefútbol account for around the same amount,

*Table 3.1* Millonarios: Financial records 1948–1952

| *Millonarios: total revenues and expenses* | | | | | |
|---|---|---|---|---|---|
| *1948–1952* | | | | | |
| *Revenues* | | | *Expenses* | | |
| *Item* | *COP* | *USD* | | *COP* | *USD* |
| Football matches (1948) | 5,52,133.11 | 2,19,973.35 | Stadium rental | 2,87,333.02 | 1,14,475.31 |
| Football matches played in Bogota (1949–1952) | 30,55,517.28 | 12,17,337.56 | Payments to Dimayor, Adefútbol and the Cundinamarca Football League | 2,02,456.25 | 80,659.86 |
| Football matches away (1949–1952) | 7,00,506.95 | 2,79,086.43 | Tickets, lodging and other expenses for visiting teams | 12,61,740.68 | 5,02,685.53 |
| **(a) Total Football matches** | **43,08,157.34** | 17,16,397.35 | Publicity and promotion | 1,53,057.81 | 60,979.21 |
| | | | Entrances, ticket offices, and security controls | 96,955.90 | 38,627.85 |
| Member fees | 90,805.69 | 36,177.57 | Referees and pitch maintenance | 32,992.52 | 13,144.43 |
| Advertisements on the field from radio broadcasts | 21,879.71 | 8,717.02 | Bonus for games won and drawn to players | 3,09,403.00 | 1,23,268.13 |
| Bus and chair rentals | 27,992.03 | 11,152.20 | Annual contract bonuses to our players | 6,71,822.08 | 2,67,658.20 |
| Sales of badges and pennants | 6,978.25 | 2,780.18 | Salaries and wages for players and administrative staff | 7,58,897.61 | 3,02,349.65 |
| Indemnities received for player injuries | 2,185.83 | 870.85 | Return tickets for players | 4,567.45 | 1,819.70 |
| Player transfer and loans | 15,900.00 | 6,334.66 | Mandatory service bonuses for players and employees | 13,667.45 | 5,445.20 |
| Lottery prices | 392.00 | 156.18 | Fees paid to professional service providers | 1,905.00 | 758.96 |
| Appreciation of investments | 330.75 | 131.77 | Travel and accommodation for Millonarios teams on tour | 56,504.35 | 22,511.69 |
| **(b) Total Other revenues** | **1,66,464.26** | 66,320.42 | Amateur football and other sports | 1,10,272.91 | 43,933.43 |
| | | | Sporting equipment | 41,807.15 | 16,656.24 |
| **Total revenues 1948–1952 (a) + (b)** | **44,74,621.60** | 17,82,717.77 | Medicines, doctors, X-rays, etc. for amateur professionals | 57,668.18 | 22,975.37 |

(*Continued*)

*Table 3.1* (Continued)

| *Millonarios: total revenues and expenses* | | | | | |
|---|---|---|---|---|---|
| *1948–1952* | | | | | |
| *Revenues* | | | *Expenses* | | |
| *Item* | *COP* | *USD* | | *COP* | *USD* |
| **Reported total revenues*** | **44,74,621.05** | 17,82,717.55 | Telephone, telegraph, and cable | 25,192.35 | 10,036.79 |
| | | | Utilities (water, electricity), janitorial services, headquarters relocation, and facility improvements | 18,477.85 | 7,361.69 |
| | | | Office supplies and expenses | 16,045.51 | 6,392.63 |
| | | | Rent paid for headquarters and bus garage | 70,170.00 | 27,956.18 |
| | | | Interests | 5,774.38 | 2,300.55 |
| | | | Collective insurance, travel insurance, etc. for personnel, employees, and players | 18,243.88 | 7,268.48 |
| | | | Contribution to the Superintendency of Corporations | 180.71 | 72.00 |
| | | | Dimayor for registering players | 2,588.32 | 1,031.20 |
| | | | Payments for player transfers | 5,867.58 | 2,337.68 |
| | | | Hospitality for sports delegations and visiting teams | 23,195.52 | 9,241.24 |
| | | | Income and wealth taxes 1948–1949 and part of ‘50 | 8,854.67 | 3,527.76 |
| | | | Statutory amortization of furniture, supplies, and bus | 24,979.96 | 9,952.18 |
| | | | Severance payments paid and accrued | 1,36,577.61 | 54,413.39 |
| | | | **Total expenses** | **44,17,199.70** | **17,59,840.52** |
| | | | **Reported total expenses*** | **44,17,304.24** | **17,59,882.17** |
| **Net income** | **57,421.90** | **22,877.25** | | | |
| **Net income reported*** | **57,316.81** | **22,835.38** | | | |

*refers to the total figures reported in the source.
***Source:*** El Tiempo, April 21, 1953, p. 10.

and that, by modern standards, Millonarios had a healthy financial situation, as player salaries, wages, and other related items accounted for 42.5% of total costs. The table also reports payments to Adefutbol, which in 1950 accounted for 5% of gate receipts.

Among the most significant debts were those owed to Dimayor, which risked blocking participation in the upcoming season. Table 3.2 reports the 1950 debts, which rose to COP 87,719.63 (USD 47,755).[49] To participate in the 1951 season, every team had to pay off its debt. Eventually, some did not make it.

Dimayor's strict enforcement penalized several clubs, but it also helped keep the organization financially viable. The 1951 season ended with the clubs owing Dimayor less than in 1950—COP 30,000 (USD 13,330)—but that figure counted Medellín's debt as an asset, leaving them space to sell its rights.[50]

Players were more lenient than Dimayor. Debt forgiveness was common practice, perhaps representing the most efficient way for players to receive at least some payment, however modest, in exchange for their freedom to seek better employment opportunities elsewhere. Not all, of course, would waive their rightful claims.

Midway between pardoning and leaving a club was the practice of issuing permits for players to go on tour with other teams. Not properly an income source for clubs, it was a temporary relief of its obligations. In 1952, for instance, while Manizales was deciding the fate of its merged team, players

*Table 3.2* Club's debt to Dimayor: 1950

| | *COP* | *USD* |
|---|---|---|
| Santa Fe | 17,180.48 | 8,765.55 |
| Sporting | 13,177.38 | 6,723.15 |
| Atlético Junior | 11,132.35 | 5,679.77 |
| Millonarios | 8,456.82 | 4,314.70 |
| Medellín | 8,430.91 | 4,301.48 |
| America | 7,130.42 | 3,637.97 |
| Universidad | 4,139.03 | 2,111.75 |
| Boca Juniors | 4,067.56 | 2,075.29 |
| Huracán | 3,002.68 | 1531.98 |
| Deportivo Cali | 2,739.38 | 1,397.64 |
| Atlético Municipal | 2,560.68 | 1,306.47 |
| Deportes Caldas | 1,642.46 | 837.99 |
| Atlético Bucaramanga | 1,098.92 | 560.67 |
| Cúcuta Deportivo | 1,092.91 | 557.61 |
| Once Deportivo | 995.73 | 508.03 |
| Deportivo Pereira | 872.02 | 444.91 |
| Total | 87,719.73 | 44,754.96 |

*Source:* Diario Gráfico, December 30, 1950, p. 21.

from the city's clubs had dispersed abroad: Concenza was playing in Brazil with Deportivo Cali, while others had joined Quindío in Venezuela.[51] Sporting, following a tour in Venezuela, followed a similar strategy. It loaned de la Hoz and Fernández to Deportivo Vasco (Venezuela), which covered their salaries while the tournament began in Colombia.[52]

Financial struggles were common. Deportivo Cali remains today one of the country's top clubs, being a significant example of the club's financial difficulties during the El Dorado era. Struggling to support its stars, on September 20, 1950, with only one matchday to go, the Superintendency of Corporations required the club to dissolve following a 50% loss of its subscribed capital.[53] With a roster full of stars and paying the annual fees in dollars in advance, the club, with a capital of COP 75,000 (USD 38,265), recorded losses of COP 72,593.03 (USD 37,037).[54] However, Cali paved the way for others to replicate in the following years. Carlos Sarmiento Angulo, the club's President, also the boss at Dimayor, dissolved the corporation and formed a new one in accordance with the regulator's requirements, while also increasing its registered capital to COP 300,000 (USD 153,060) in January 1951.[55] That solution would be short-lived. Before the start of the 1952 season, following losses of COP150,000 (USD 76760), Sarmiento announced in January that he had liquidated all his positions in the club.[56] He never really left. Before the year was over, he was running the club again.

The problems with Cali, the club, and Cali the city were almost structural. The total gate receipts during the 1951 season added to COP 900,000 (USD 418,000) for América, Cali, and Boca Juniors. The figure represented the estimated costs for the three clubs—COP 400,000 (USD 186,000) for Deportivo Cali, COP 300,000 (USD 139,500) for Boca Juniors, and COP 200,000 (USD 93,000) for América.[57] However, as Table 3.1 reports, the expenditure column is extensive. In Cali, on top of salaries and bonuses, each club had to pay 14% of its receipts to the Physical Education commission, which pushed the clubs into deficit after adding stadium rent and other expenses.

In May 1952, the regional government decided to aid the Cali clubs. It reduced the tax on the Physical Education commission to 6% and decreed that the maximum stadium rental would be 6% if gate receipts exceeded COP 20,000 (USD 9,300) and the games were category 1, and 5% if they were category 2. It correspondingly allowed increasing ticket prices in the stadium's shadow area (east stands) to COP 4 (USD 1,9) and COP 6 (USD 2,8), but the latter, category 1 games, could be limited to only 4 per year.[58]

Cali's financial problems were not over. Unhappy with the situation in the city, eager to exploit the new Medellin football stadium, Omar Méndez, Calí's general manager, successfully negotiated to relocate the club for the 1953 season. Cali played its first home game of the season (matchday 3) in Medellin on May 3, 1953. With gate receipts of COP 20,000 (USD 9,300), Pereira drew 2-2 in the only home game Cali played in Medellin. Weeks later, the governor transferred COP 60,000 (USD 27,900), convincing the board to remain in Cali.[59]

It is ironic that Cali sought to relocate to Medellin, when shortly before, as the Medellin clubs faced dissolution, they had threatened to move to Cali. Until the inauguration of the Atanasio Girardot stadium in March 1953, Medellin lacked a proper stadium, forcing the teams to play on a horse racing track. They still had to pay a fee, which, given the attendance figures, impacted the balance sheets. In 1950, when the three teams were still in competition, the rental fee was 10% of gross gate receipts (up from 7% in 1949), except for Huracán, which played for free on Saturdays.[60] The lack of proper infrastructure led Medellín to consider moving to Palmira, near Cali, in 1951.[61]

Attendance was thus a significant problem, particularly for Huracán, which played on Saturdays and generated gate receipts that rarely exceeded COP 5,000 (USD 2,325). According to the contemporary press, for a COP 5,000 game, in 1951, the costs amounted to COP 3,021 (USD 1,405), excluding salaries and bonuses—the latter of which could rise to COP 1,000 (USD 465) in case of a victory.[62] Huracán had problems paying its players, forcing most Peruvians and Uruguayans to leave by the end of the first half of the 1951 season. On the brink of dissolution, some backers saved the season, keeping the team running. Huracán would, nevertheless, disappear by 1953.

It was common, as early as 1951, to default on salaries. In May 1951, before a game against América, Medellín players issued an ultimatum: they would not play unless the club paid the overdue wages.[63] The club did not pay, but it convinced them to play by asking the fans for support. Only 5,000 fans attended, with a meager gate receipt of COP 3,000 (USD 1,395), leading Federico Kan and Alejandro Caño, the team's main backers, to ask Dimayor for help.[64] The club prevented the strike, but problems would eventually surface back.

During the 1951 season recess, Medellín declared bankruptcy, which led Dimayor to step in to administer the club. Dimayor agreed to back the team to avoid further disruptions to the tournament, while promising to honor the players' contracts.[65] However, by late June, Dimayor announced that it would negotiate the club's registration to cover the debts to players and other providers.[66]

Still, players and other employees were not receiving their payments. In despair, Agapito Perales, the coach, representing the players, wrote in July to the Minister of Justice asking for his intervention to secure the players' payments, as, with the society liquidated, they had nowhere to go and claim all or part of the COP 46,537.32 (USD 21,645) that the club owed them in salaries and bonuses.[67] Days earlier, the Peruvian players had written to the Peruvian Minister of Foreign Relations stating that they wanted to return home but were impeded by Medellín, and later by Dimayor.

The players claimed that Medellín F.B.C., as the now-dissolved society was known, had revenues in 1950 of COP 216,000 (USD 100,465) from home games, COP 69,000 (USD 32,093) from away games, and COP 10,000 (USD

4,650) from friendlies. In meetings held in mid-July 1951 between Dimayor and the players, the latter defended that the expenses could not have exceeded COP 100,000 (USD 46,511).

Dimayor administered the club, paying the players COP 20,000 at the beginning of the second half of the 1951 season, and promising the rest by the end of the season.[68] In the end, Medellín survived, finished third-to-last, and by November, once the season had finished, Dimayor attempted to sell the club's rights for COP 50,000 (USD 23,255). The club did not participate in the 1952 and 1953 leagues.

The story of Atlético Nacional, until July 1950 known as Atlético Municipal, is that of an outsider. With the country full of foreign stars, the club played only with Colombians under the motto "the team that always plays at home". The decision came at a cost, as the team's performance did little to draw significant crowds. In 1950, the club called on the city and its thriving economy for support. Powerful entrepreneurs stepped in. Atlético Nacional was formally established on August 4, 1950, with an authorized capital of COP 250,000, when the Board of Directors, comprising prominent Antioquia businessmen.[69]

In the 1952 season, financial distress forced the club to call for help again. Nacional organized a civic week on April 1 with reports announcing that Leticia Fabric Factory contributed COP 1,000 (USD 465).[70] Overall, the initiative came to nothing. A benefit concert scheduled for April 19th fell apart after the singers pulled out at the last minute. At that point, Nacional was requesting an exemption from paying the 4% of gate receipts that each team had to pay Dimayor for every home game.[71] Nacional languished in the lower half of the table, ultimately forcing the club to sign foreign players in 1953, just as the El Dorado era was drawing to a close.

The Cali clubs also faced persistent financial difficulties—an irony, since the powerhouses of the time were Millonarios, Deportivo Cali, and Boca Juniors, with Cúcuta and Santa Fe sometimes included in that tier.[72] Boca Juniors' problems stem from playing on Saturdays, which directly affected attendance. Thus, during the entire period, Boca constantly complained about it and tried to move its games to Sundays.

The cash shortage became a structural issue for Boca, which implemented almost every action in the playbook to pay its Paraguayan stars. In February, before the 1951 season, the President, Aníbal Aguirre Arías, pardoned a COP 6,000 (USD 3,060) debt the club owed him and lent an additional COP 4,000 (USD 2,040). Other stockholders also invested in acquiring further shares, up to COP 1,000 per share.[73] Still, just a month later, Boca was overdue on payments, and its Paraguayan players were threatening to leave.[74] The team, with a starting lineup of ten Paraguayans and one Colombian (Canino Caicedo), managed to negotiate the payment of COP 20,000 (USD 9,300) out of the COP 30,000 (USD 13,935) they owed to guarantee they would fly to Medellin to play. Boca Juniors, without Paraguayans, was literally nothing.

As the 1952 season approached, in agreement with their players, the club reduced monthly salaries by 25% and bonuses by 35%.[75] Revenue-wise, the season began poorly for every team, as the Copa Colombia collected just COP 60,000 (USD 27,900) across seven games. The figure implied that, while debts continued to pile up, given the tournament rules, each team received, on average, just around COP 4,300 (USD 1,990). Boca Juniors owed José Ocampos and Negri, among other players, and coach Miguel Ortega COP 11,000 (USD 5,115), including overdue salaries and bonuses. Despite the cuts in their contract renewals, Centurión, López, Genes, Negri, Cañete, A. Berní, E. Berní, Ocampos, Goretta, and Rolón did not receive a single peso when official football began, but by then, the Paraguayans were partners in administering the club.[76]

Approaching matchday 1, Ocampos and Ortega refused to fly to Manizales unless the club paid them. Boca's reaction, perhaps hurt by the 4-1 defeat against Deportivo Manizales, was out of proportion: it called on the Colombian government to expel Ocampos and Ortega from the country.[77] The Paraguayan embassy, pressed by the press back home who had headlines stating "you are not alone", contacted the Colombian Minister of Foreign Relations, asking the government to enforce their labor rights. Meanwhile, Dimayor supported Boca, stating that the club had already paid 57,286 COP (26,640) to its players in 1952, that the amount owed was a small remnant of the previous year's bonuses, and that the explanation was the excessively long recess in Colombian football.[78]

Boca, like every other team, wanted to play the first home game of the season, either in Copa Colombia or the league, against Millonarios, hoping to raise significant funds to clear debts. Boca faced Quindío in Cali for the first round of Copa Colombia. Lucky them, however, their first home league game, on matchday 3 was against Millonarios. The gate receipt of COP 55,000 (USD 25,580) topped that of the least popular team in Cali, América, which on matchday one had revenues of COP 38,000 (USD 17,670) when Millonarios visited.

To solve Boca's puzzle, all parties, Dimayor, the players, and the club, used the gate receipts from the Millonarios game as collateral. On Friday, April 25, a week before Millonarios' visit, all parties agreed that Boca would immediately pay COP 5,000 (USD 2,325) to the players and that the proceeds from the game with Millonarios would be used to pay the remainder. Those who had refused to play, the agreement continued, would not receive salary payments for those eight days of strike.[79]

The schedule called for Boca to visit Millonarios on September 21, a second-round fixture. With the latter undefeated, seven points ahead, the former was among the few teams that could spark interest in the season's outcome. José Ocampo, the center half, with skills as a labor union leader, posed another challenge to the league by announcing that unless Millonarios paid upfront COP 15,000 (USD 6,980), they would not play. The attitude was ill-received, and the number was out of proportion, because Millonarios' only obligation was to pay Boca the usual COP 1,500 (USD 698).

Ocampo justified his request, pointing out that Boca owed the Paraguayan players COP 30,000 (USD 13,950) while they were only receiving COP 500 (USD 232) a month. He added that he was just "asking for a favor" because Millonarios was the only club that could afford to lend them money.[80] In exchange, he promised they would play a Boca–Millonarios friendly, the location of which was unclear, because, according to Ocampo, the money was to buy tickets to fly back home. Days later, he further clarified his position.

Ocampo claimed that on August 31, following the agreement reached months earlier, the club had committed to pay USD 6,000. It also owed bonuses for games won and tied, around COP 450 (USD 209) per player. The debt, he added, was guaranteed by a promissory note signed in front of Dimayor and the Paraguayan ambassador, but the former appropriated the notes, leaving the players with nothing but the ambassador's knowledge of their existence. Including what the club would have to pay them on December 31, Boca owed around COP 47,000 (USD 21,860). Still, Ocampo continued, the players agreed to receive just COP 20,000 (9,300) and their salaries. Lastly, he added, the COP 15,000 (USD 6,980) were contingent on a Boca–Millonarios match, which should generate enough cash to purchase the tickets back home.[81]

Following the playbook and with most of the Paraguayans gone, Boca established a new organization just a month later, with the ten founding partners contributing COP 10,000 (USD 4,650) each. Anibal Aguirre, of course, was the president of the new company.[82] Boca, now with only five Paraguayans, finished second in 1952, despite playing with a majority of Colombians. However, the club incurred losses of COP 18,000 (USD 8,372), and in January 1953, Aguirre threatened to move the team to Medellin while seeking additional partners.[83] Boca remained in Cali, managed to play on Sundays because of América's withdrawal, but, structurally in debt, it finally disappeared after the 1957 season.

América completed its El Dorado experience before the era was over. Its players refused to play the final game of the 1951 season due to unpaid salaries. To avoid further sanctions from Dimayor, América sent the amateur team to play against Junior in Barranquilla. They lost 4-0, and the absence of the professional squad significantly reduced attendance. Only 1,834 people attended, leaving gate receipts of just COP 840 (USD 335). Even the manager, the Peruvian Adelfo Magallanes, complained. He had left Alianza Lima in January 1951 following an offer of USD 2,500 (or USD 1,500 according to contemporary press), a monthly salary of COP 700 (USD 358), plus COP 60 (USD 31) per game won, and COP 30 (USD 15) for a draw. As of December 1951, the club owed him USD 1,800 from the signing fee, plus three months' salary and bonuses.[84] The crisis continued in the 1952 season when, even before the season started, it already owed COP 16,000 (USD 6,375) to

Dimayor and an additional COP 7,000 (USD 2,788) to the other clubs in the league. Things, nevertheless, could get worse.

As part of its Colombian tour, Boca Juniors (ARG), hired by Boca Juniors and América, agreed to play the latter in Cali on December 14, 1952. With the stadium packed for over an hour, the América players sat on the pitch, legs crossed, demanding that the club for pay.

On Friday, before the game, the players asked Manuel Correa Valencia, president, general manager, and treasurer of América, to pay them the COP 7,200 (USD 2,868) that the club owed them. By 3 p.m. on Sunday, just before the game, Correa promised COP 3,000 (USD 1,195). At capacity, the stadium meant gate receipts were more than enough to pay the players' debt; they knew this. Indeed, revenues reached COP 18,550 (USD 7,390), so América had no alternative but to pay the players the COP 7,200 (USD 2,869) they were asking for.[85]

Tension was in the air. Before canceling the debt, the speaker announced through the stadium loudspeakers that Dimayor had suspended the match because América was not up to date with its payments. They added, with a typical regionalist sentiment, that in the morning Millonarios had played against Huracán (ARG) despite owing COP 15,000 (USD 5,976), "further proof of Dimayor's aberrant persecution against provincial teams".[86]

América was now ready to play, but Boca Juniors grew nervous. The Argentines, worried about their payment, have now requested payment of COP 11,000 (USD 4,383) upfront. The situation escalated when Cali's Government Secretary ordered the imprisonment of the Argentines on charges that will never be clear. After tense negotiations, the game finally took place. Boca Juniors defeated América 2–4.

América not only owed the players. Days later, Dimayor suspended América and froze the players' passes, hinting that they would transfer them to recover the money the club owed the organization. Meanwhile, in Cali, América's board saw this as a Deportivo Cali and Boca Juniors maneuver to vanish the club, with the support of other big teams waiting to land players such as Felix Castillo or Rigoberto Felandro on their rosters.

América was unable to pay its debts to Dimayor, and Castillo left for Alianza Lima, while Felandro moved to the rising Venezuelan league. The club was unable to participate in the 1953 season and rejoined in 1954. It would not become a significant force in Colombian and South American football until the influx of drug money from the Rodríguez Orejuela brothers in the late 1970s and 1980s.

The crisis impacted almost every club, including the first champion. Santa Fe pursued alternative revenue streams, charging members a monthly fee that granted them access to club infrastructure and admission to games. For the 1950 season, category A members (those attending the Western stands of the stadium) paid a monthly fee of COP 12 (USD 6,12). The club reduced the fee to COP 8 (USD 4,08) in 1951, canceling the benefit that allowed its members to buy additional tickets at half price.

Still, as Table 3.2 reports, Santa Fe was the most indebted team to Dimayor by the end of the 1950 season, owing almost half of the COP 150,000 (USD 76,530) in capital it had in 1949.[87] The English player's import, at a cost of COP 86,000 (USD 43,877), negatively impacted the balance sheet. The 1950 season finished with a COP 135,000 (USD 68,870) deficit, despite revenues of COP 800,000 (USD 408,160) and having paid COP 300,000 (USD 153,060) in salaries and bonuses.[88]

Dimayor had to become imaginative to ease the club's debts. In an odd decision, during the January 1951 assembly, Dimayor determined that to participate in the upcoming season, the clubs should pay 100% of the debt if they owed less than COP 1,000, 25% if the debt was between COP 1,000 and COP 5,000, 35% for a debt ranging from COP 5,000 to COP 10,000 and 50% if the club owed more than COP 10,000. According to Dimayor's calculations, the first installment would amount to COP 36,322.30 (USD 18,532), leaving a balance of COP 45,625 (USD 23,278) guaranteed through promissory notes.[89] The last three teams to pay were Santa Fe, Junior, and Sporting, which paid on March 2, 1951, after Dimayor released the season schedule, excluding them from the draw.[90]

Santa Fe never fully recovered from the English players' investment debacle during this era. The financial statements in mid-October 1951 revealed a worrisome situation in which the club's liabilities of COP 350,000 (USD 139,442) had exceeded its capital of COP 150,000 (USD 59,761), resulting in a COP 140,000 (USD 55,776) debt to the players. To address the situation, the assembly agreed to offer the players COP 60,000 (USD 23,904) through a future issuance of 30,000 shares, valued at the current price of COP 5 (USD 2) per share. Adding to this, COP 150,000 (USD 59,761), the club would raise COP 20,000 (USD 7,968) by selling 1,000 season tickets for 20 games.[91]

The plan did not work. On October 30, 1951, Independiente Santa Fe was officially dissolved despite having only a few matchdays remaining in the tournament, which the team nonetheless completed. The outgoing board and the players, who were cooperative throughout the process, eventually agreed that 60% of gate receipts would go to pay salaries and bonuses, 20% to pay debts owed to players originated before November 1951, and the rest to satisfy other provisions.[92] The assembly agreed to establish a new society called Deportivo Santa Fe, with a capital of COP 200,000 (USD 79,681), to begin operations around December 1.[93]

The new Santa Fe organized a 1952 preseason tour of Ecuador and Central America with its star players to raise money to pay off old Santa Fe's debts. However, the club announced that upon return, all players would be free to move.[94] Many players, with Santa Fe unable to offer competitive salaries, would wind up at Universidad, including Ángel Perucca, Luis López, Arnaldo, Marío Fernández Martínez, and the Spanish coach José Castillo.[95] With the club having lost many of its star players, Hernando Carrillo, Enrique Rodríguez Nieto, Bernardo Bustamante, and Guillermo Bustamante purchased the team's registration from Dimayor for COP 50,000 (USD 19,920) in a bid to retain those who remained.[96]

Unfortunately, both Rial and Pontoni refused the COP 12,000 (USD 4,781) offered to renew with Santa Fe.[97] Rial left for Nacional (URU), where he played before moving to Real Madrid once San Lorenzo received ARS 230,000 (USD 16,400) from the Uruguayans.[98] That he left for UYU 700 (USD 262) plus bonuses per point won says a lot about Colombia's credibility.[99] Under the Lima Agreement, Portuguesa de Desportos (São Paulo) paid San Lorenzo COP 20,000 (USD 9,300) for the transfer of Pontoni to Brazil.[100] For the 1952 season, Santa Fe lost all its stars, even as its 1951 players forgave around COP 100,000 (USD 39,840).[101] The former champion made the 1952 season debut in the Copa Colombia with half the squad composed of amateurs, and finished the league in an ignominious ninth place.

The new board made new investments, but with the 1952 season over, the Bustamante brothers retired and negotiated a price with Carillo for their stakes. However, Santa Fe performed brilliantly in the 1953 preseason friendlies, beating Cali, Millonarios, Rapid Vienna (AUT), and Independiente (ARG), and drawing with River Plate (ARG). The Bustamante brothers felt the negotiated price was unfair and asked for a correction, but Carrillo and Rodríguez refused.[102] The corresponding lawsuit put the club at risk of dissolving again. Fortunately, the parties reached an agreement just days before the 1953 season began. The crisis was over, but so were the days when Santa Fe could have a Perucca, a Rial, a Mitten, and a Pontoni simultaneously wearing the red jersey. The team finished the 1953 season playing with only Colombian players.

Universidad, the third team of Bogota, faced the same difficulties as its peers. In 1951, with little debt but only four players under contract after a firing frenzy in July, the club faced complications in assembling a competitive roster for the second leg of the tournament. Following a defeat to Deportivo Cali a month earlier, in May 1951, the board threatened to fire Colombo and Rosales, but only a recent signing, José Coccellato, was fired. The firing frenzy exploded in July when the principal stockholders, Marco Alzate Avendaño and Daniel Hoyos Robledo, fired the Panamanian, Gerardo Warren, the Hungarian goalkeeper, Wladislav Monsider, Mario Bassano, and the Argentines Calistro, Miranda, and Rosales, plus the Colombians Luis Rubio, "Buche" Orozco, Quijano, and Talero.

They literally fired the entire team except for four: the Argentine Botero, and the Costa Ricans Mario Murillo, Maximilian Villalobos, and Umaña. The solution came from its rivals when, in a dubious move, several teams sent bench players. Universidad finished the 1951 season in second-to-last place. For the 1952 season, the last of its existence, they brought in players from Bucaramanga and Santa Fe to complete the roster, finishing in 10th place.[103]

Three teams from Barranquilla represented El Dorado; none of them survived. The first team to retire not only from the Caribbean capital but also from the Dimayor league was Deportivo Barranquilla in 1949. On September 10, days before matchday 18, the team announced that it would retire from the league. Dimayor later declared that they had learnt the team had been sold, but they could not contact the new owner. They were trying to find a way to help the team, but the effort was fruitless.[104] Deportivo Barranquilla retired, but did so with the intention of attracting attendance and minimizing expenses by playing friendlies in Barranquilla. On Thursday, 22, 1949, for instance, they played and lost to Barcelona (Ecuador) before 2,674 fans, for a meager revenue of COP 4,249 (USD 2,168).[105] We have five other friendlies registered that year, all in Barranquilla, but eventually the team disappeared. Indeed, the low level of attendance was a constant issue in Barranquilla. During the 1950 preseason, Junior played five home games, but, to the club's despair, total gate receipts reached only COP 39,000 (USD 19,900), insufficient to support the team in its upcoming reentry to the professional league.[106]

Sporting and Junior were chronically in debt to Dimayor (Table 3.2) and, as mentioned earlier, were even cut from the season draw weeks before the start of the 1951 season. Junior generated COP 350,000 (USD 178,571) in revenues during the 1950 season, but it still lost COP 12,000 (USD 6,122). To cover its losses, the club borrowed COP 10,000 (USD 5,102) from its backers. It is not clear who precisely gave the money, but some of the board members were recognized politicians (Ernest McCausland) and entrepreneurs (Julio Mario Santodomingo).[107]

Not a year had passed when, at the dawn of the 1952 season, the Sporting and Junior players combined forces and refused to play because they were not being paid. On matchday one in 1952, up to eight Sporting players declined to fly to Bogota to play Santa Fe, while Junior, which played at home against Atlético Nacional, had five players refusing to play.[108] Junior argued that it was only late in paying one fortnight, but Sporting owed COP 13,000 (USD 5,179) to at least eight of its players. Sporting lost 2-1 to Santa Fe on matchday 1 after fielding an unprecedented lineup: just two foreigners, Chompi Henríquez and Di Gregorio, in the starting eleven. The club and players reached an agreement under which the former would release the players' transfers if it failed to deliver. The formula, backed by Dimayor, was not universally accepted. Benjamin Pellegrino, Juan Carlos Carrera, Aldo Ottagio, and Amadeo Colangelo refused to accept the agreement, which forced the club to pay them the COP 2,000 (USD 797) it owed and, nevertheless, release their transfer passes.[109]

Sporting slowly but surely disappeared despite having enough players, mostly Colombians, for the second half of the 1952 season. In April 1953, together with Universidad and Manizales, they got excluded from the tournament for lacking a team, although they eventually managed to register for the 1953 season. Junior, meanwhile, competed with dignity, finishing eighth out of twelve teams, with mostly Colombians. Eventually, both clubs disappeared. Junior would return 12 years later, in 1966.

The other Caribbean team, Samarios from Santa Marta, which joined professionalism in 1951 with grand objectives, received initial support from important local firms: COP 65,000 (USD 30,230).[110] The club finished the 1951 season with a debt of COP 40,000 (USD 15,936).[111] In 1952, despite further investment, including from Dávila e Hijos and other local business-people, the club was bound to disappear. In September, the game between Samarios and Bucaramanga got canceled because Negrescu placed a lien on the gate receipts due to unpaid wages, and the club could not afford the COP 1,500 (US 698) that, under Dimayor regulations, they had to pay the away team. Samarios lost that game; it managed to finish the season, but by the end of the year, the clash between players and club was unsustainable. The financial situation and the lack of support were such that, on the second-to-last matchday, on December 3, 1952, Deportivo Samarios preferred to play its home game vs América in Cali. The last official game played at home in Santa Marta was on November 9, losing 11 to 1 with Quindío.

The Samarios case provides an excellent illustration of how club management understood its relationship with players. By the end of the year, the club was bitterly complaining about allegations made by several of its players. Fuzessy claimed that the club owed him COP 2,500 (USD 996), while the club maintained it owed "only" COP 470 (USD 187), adding that he, along with Bruno and Contin, had abandoned the team following their crushing defeat to Millonarios in Bogota (4-0) in late November. Carlos Bernier, the club's general manager, acknowledged that the debt to Contin and Bruno was approximately what they claimed (COP 2,827—USD 1,126), but argued that "more than 70% of that debt" predated August.[112] The implication seemed to be that older debts somehow carried less weight than recent ones and that the players should accept a certain level of debt.

Bernier further blamed the players for the club's inability to generate greater revenues, describing their performances as "abysmal and shameful". Nevertheless, he claimed that despite the players having unilaterally broken their contracts, the club was working to fulfill its obligations "to the extent possible".[113] Bernier highlighted Rossi's case as exemplary. Over the course of that season, Rossi received just COP 400 (USD 159) of the COP 2,550 (USD 1,016) he was owed through December. Bernier praised Rossi's conduct because the player had forgiven COP 1,550 (USD 618) and accepted payment of the remaining COP 600 (USD 239) in convenient installments. In other words, players who demanded their wages were condemned, while those who forgave debts were praised. Severance costs for Samarios, with its roster full of Europeans, came with an extra load as they had to purchase return tickets to the Old Continent. Regarding Fuzessy, Bernier congratulated himself on securing his passage to Europe by sea.[114] One assumes the ship didn't sail all the way to Hungary.

The teams in the coffee region followed different paths. In 1950, Deportes Caldas surprised the world by winning the league. It has been lost in time, however, that in the same season, Once Deportivo finished last. Manizales' market was not large enough to hold two competitive teams. Thus, it is no surprise that Deportivo Manizales emerged as the city's sole team when, for the 1952 season, the two clubs merged.

Supported by various backers, including the municipality, which during 1952 paid ten installments of COP 1,000 (USD 465), Deportivo Manizales entered the league.[115] The situation in the new club was chaotic from the beginning. Already, for matchday 1, Navarro and Ávila refused to play, arguing that the club was not complying with their contracts. They did play, but by the end of the week, board members Eduardo Gómez Arrubla and Gustavo Gutiérrez were threatening to resign.[116] The team finished 12 out of 15 clubs and, lacking attendance and support, released all its players on December 1, 1952.

Pereira represents an example of players blending with the community to such an extent that they forgave significant debts. During the 1951 end-of-year friendly season, the Peruvian champions, Sport Boys, played Deportivo Cali in Cali before 8,000 fans and Millonarios in Bogota before 15,000. When the Peruvians arrived in Pereira, however, the 7,000 fans that attended the game were not enough to avoid a net loss of COP 1,500 (USD 598). The club, given the lack of support from city officials and fans, threatened to dissolve and liquidate the society even before the year ended.[117] Before the 1952 season started, the club announced its dissolution again, now with a more tangible problem: owing COP 1,547 (USD 616) to Dimayor, a payment necessary to participate in the upcoming season.[118] Having to pay before the end of February, the club's executive director, Rogerio Vélez Isaza, met on the 28th with the city's mayor to ask for support in buying the necessary tickets to send the Paraguayans back home.

But the unexpected happened. At the last minute, from Armenia, the city known as "the Miracle City", Quindío extended the necessary help to Pereira. The Armenian club had just successfully participated in an international tournament in Caracas (Venezuela), playing six games. It thus had the resources to step in and help the club from the neighboring city of Pereria by paying the money. It was a way to pay a moral debt, because Pereira's vote ultimately allowed Quindío to enter Dimayor for the 1951 season. The clubs agreed to play two games—one in Pereira and one in Armenia—to fund each team's treasury further. Weeks later, on March 9, 1951, Quindío traveled to Pereira to play a friendly, which successfully raised COP 11,000 (USD 5,612) thanks to the 5,000 fans who enthusiastically attended to show their support for Pereira. Although we find no explicit reports, one might assume that Pereira paid Quindío the debt with cash from that game.

Pereira's problems, however, were chronic. By the end of the 1952 season in December, Pereira owed its players over COP 35,000 (USD 13,944), and with no plans to play friendlies before the following season, the club was facing dissolution.[119] Two months later, the situation worsened; Pereira owed its Paraguayan players COP 50,000 (USD 19,920).

In an unexpected turn of events, the players wrote a letter stating that

> the club owes us (…) COP 50,000, which means that if we were to demand payment of such an amount, the team, our beloved Deportivo Pereira, could not survive and would have to disappear from the sporting scene

> of this gracious Colombia. Such a sad and regrettable event will not occur through any fault of ours.

They continued by stating that "despite playing the final months of last year's championship in precarious conditions (…), we managed to place Pereira's name in an enviable position among Colombia's professional teams, having secured third place (…)". They concluded:

> We Paraguayans of Deportivo Pereira are noble and love Pereira and Colombia as we love our Paraguay, and just as our ancestors knew sacrifice in the Chaco War, we too, on an infinitely smaller scale, wish to make a gesture that hardly qualifies as sacrifice: WE DECLARE CANCELED THE DEBT that Deportivo Pereira has contracted with us. The team owes us nothing; we owe the city our gratitude for its generosity and boundless hospitality. We exchange money for sincerity and kindness. The balance is gratifyingly in our favor.[120]

The Paraguayans saved Pereira for one year. The team finished second-to-last in 1953 and disappeared before the 1954 tournament.

Quindío, with a brand-new stadium in Armenia, inaugurated in March 1951, successfully navigated the crisis. The stadium, packed, could fit around 25,000 fans as it did on October 14, 1951, when Millonarios visited and defeated Quindío 0–4. The gate receipts of COP 50,800 (USD 20,239) were only comparable to those on big nights in Bogota and Cali. Importantly, it was not a spur-of-the-moment.

Probably because of the stadium, Quindío had decent revenue figures, averaging gate receipts of COP 15,200 (USD 6,055) per game in 1951. It complemented this source of income with the 1952 tour in Venezuela and the ability to bring top Argentine clubs to Armenia. In December, Quindío played in Armenia against both Boca Juniors (ARG) and Huracán (ARG). It defeated the former 2-1 for gate receipts of COP 13,000 (USD 5,179). Quindío is probably the hidden pearl of El Dorado. It finished 5th in 1951 and 1952, runner-up in 1953 and 1954, and went on to win the league in 1956.

In the Northeast, the two teams had very different objectives. While Bucaramanga's bid for glory fell short, Cucuta fielded a squad that included World Champions. As in other smaller teams, low attendance was the driving force behind Bucaramanga's financial troubles. Following the trend, Millonarios' visit was key to adjusting its balance sheet. In 1951, Millonarios agreed to play a friendly match in Bucaramanga two days after the official league game, implying, presumably, a significant investment. The official game, played on August 5, ended in defeat (1–2), but left the club with COP 12,000 (USD 4,780). The friendly left the club with a "ridiculous gate receipt" of COP 1,400 (USD 558), leaving them on shaky financial ground and forcing them to play the following home game on the away turf, facing Sporting in Barranquilla.[121]

Millonarios' game was the last resort following Atlético Bucaramanga's general manager announcement in June 1951 that the club was unable to fulfill its obligations to foreign players, paving the way for its liquidation.[122] Still, in November, they managed to organize a tour in Aruba and Curazao, where they received COP 3,000 (USD 1,195) for each of the three games, although unfortunately, we have no records of the scores.[123]

The club designed different survival strategies in November 1951, such as launching a campaign to popularize the club and establishing a membership system, seeking contributions to ensure sufficient cash flow.[124] The club dissolved in December and released most of its players, many of whom moved to Universidad for the 1952 season. Bucaramanga was unable to register in time for the 1952 season because the old society owed Dimayor COP 771,25 (USD 359).[125]

To cut costs, Bucaramanga innovatively published an ad in the newspapers seeking professional football players willing to play for a monthly salary, with no bonuses.[126] The ad worked, and they competed, but in football, money is quality: Bucaramanga finished last in the 1952 and 1953 seasons and retired for 1954.

Cúcuta assembled a team to win the title. Unlike others, attendance responded in its first year in the league, which probably motivated its move toward Uruguayan players in 1951. In December 1950, although the club had some overdue salary payments, it borrowed COP 10,000 (USD 5,102) from the incoming Board of Directors while also increasing its capital to COP 100,000 (USD 51,020).[127]

Cúcuta finished third in 1951, but as the new season approached, the club was feeling the strain of having top-quality footballers, forcing it to devise a novel approach to generate extra funding. With this in mind, they decided, in February 1952, to hold a civic week, which included bazaars, raffles, and the collection of an extra transit tax as official aid.[128] The results were disappointing. With revenues of COP 16,616 (USD 6,620) and costs of COP 6,300 (USD 2,510), the civic week left the club just over COP 10,000 (USD 3,984).[129] Despite the effort, cutting costs remained a necessity. Thus, by March, allegedly due to their low performance, Cúcuta fired the Uruguayans Ángel Otero, Abrahan Gonzalez, and Juan José Tulic.[130] However, just days later, the goalkeeper Di Marco broke his clavicle and a rib, forcing Cúcuta to bring back Tulic.

Later, in October, the club fired two other Uruguayans, Ramón Alberto Villaverde and Washington Barrios. The same Villaverde who, a couple of years later, after a stint at Millonarios, played nine seasons at Barcelona (ESP). It seems evident that firing Villaverde had nothing to do with his performance. Quite the opposite—he was a fan favorite in Cúcuta. As it happened, Villaverde placed a judicial lien on the gate receipts from the September 28 match against Millonarios, which brought in COP 23,000 (USD 9,163), to collect on a debt of COP 2,500 (USD 996). The club paid its debt and handed over its transfer papers.[131]

To save the club, in the last quarter of 1952, Cúcuta dissolved its corporation and created a Provisional Board, but, in the absence of a leader, three journalists took over the team's management. [132] This action proved the team's importance to the community while also reflecting the local elites' lack of interest. The club paid all its debts to obtain Dimayor's permit to play in Central America between January and February 1953. Cúcuta survived, finished sixth out of twelve teams, but was financially unviable and retired for the 1954 season.

It was common practice for clubs to default on payments. They tend to fight back against players, even when they explicitly accept their debts. In this struggle, Dimayor permanently backed clubs and praised players for forgiving debts, a sign of the contemporary approach between firms and workers.

The recount reveals a previously unknown framework in which most of the clubs were in dire financial straits as early as 1950. Millonarios stood as El Dorado's flagship, excelling both on the pitch and in its finances, but it was an exception. The clubs opted to follow Millonarios' outstanding results, but neither the market nor the executive managers had the scale or the ability to replicate the strategy. Overall, even from the start, El Dorado was financially unsustainable in the long run, if not in the short run.

## Notes

1 Diario Gráfico, December 15, 1950, p. 8, and El Tiempo, December 15, 1950, p. 10.
2 The detailed story is described in Potts Harmer (2019), pp. 148–152.
3 Diario Gráfico, March 2, 1951, p. 8.
4 Potts Harmer (2019), p. 153 and El Tiempo, July 9, 1950, p. 8.
5 Potts Harmer (2019), p. 153.
6 Potts Harmer (2019), p. 155.
7 Immigration records, Archivo General de la Nación (Bogota-Colombia).
8 Adamson (1996), p. 146.
9 Adamson (1996), p. 160.
10 Adamson (1996), p. 165.
11 El Tiempo, August 17, 1951, p. 8.
12 La Crónica, February 14, 1951, p. 8.
13 La Crónica, February 16, 1951, p. 4.
14 La Crónica, February 17, 1951, p. 6.
15 La Crónica, February 22, 1951, p. 4.
16 La Crónica, March 1, 1951, p. 4.
17 La Crónica, October 18, 1951, p. 5.
18 La Crónica, April 5, 1951, p. 8, and La Crónica, April 9, 1951, p. 5.
19 La Crónica, November 22, 1951, p. 6.
20 Diario Gráfico, March 14, 1951, p. 20.
21 La Crónica, March 19, 1951, p. 8.
22 La Crónica, April 24,1951, p. 5.
23 El Heraldo, June 20, 1950, p. 9.
24 El Tiempo, June 25, 1950, p. 11.
25 El Heraldo, October 28, 1950, p. 9.
26 El Heraldo, November 8, 1950, p. 7.

27 El Tiempo, December 2, 1950, p. 6.
28 El Heraldo, November 21, 1950, p. 6.
29 El Tiempo, December 3, 1950, p. 11.
30 El Heraldo, April 24, 1951, p. 9.
31 EL Mundo Deportivo, April 4, 1951, p. 1.
32 El Mundo Deportivo, April 5, 1951, p. 11.
33 Diario Gráfico, April 7, 1951, p. 5.; Diario Gráfico April 11, 1951, p. 6; El Heraldo, April 14, 1951, p. 8.
34 Revista Goles, No 145, p. 3 & 12. El Heraldo, April 12, 1951, p. 9.
35 El Heraldo, April 9, 1951, p. 8.
36 Diario Gráfico, August 16, 1951, pp. 1, 19.
37 El Tiempo, August 21, 1951, p. 9.
38 Diario Gráfico, September 12, 1951, p. 16.
39 Diario Gráfico, September 13, 1951, p. 1.
40 Diario Gráfico, October 12, 1951, p. 1.
41 La Crónica, October 23, 1951, p. 5.
42 Revista Goles, December 27, pp. 28–29.
43 El Comercio—Lima, October 26, 1951, p. 20.
44 La Crónica, October 25, 1951, p. 8.
45 La Crónica, October 25, 1951, p. 3.
46 Revista Goles No. 248, p. 8.
47 Revista Goles No. 307, p. 8.
48 El Heraldo, January 10, 1950, p. 9.
49 Diario Gráfico, December 30, 1950, p. 21.
50 Diario Gráfico, December 12, 1951, p. 19.
51 El Tiempo, February 5, 1952, p. 10.
52 Diario Gráfico, February 8, 1952, p. 18.
53 El Heraldo, September 20, 1950, p. 9 & Diario Gráfico, September 22, 1950, p. 20.
54 El Heraldo, September 22, 1950, p. 8.
55 Diario Gráfico, January 18, 1951, p. 21.
56 Diario Gráfico, January 10, 1952, p. 19 and El Tiempo, January 10, 1952, p. 10.
57 Diario Gráfico, December 11, 1951, p. 20.
58 Diario Gráfico, May 9, 1952, p. 18.
59 El Tiempo, May 29, 1953, p. 10.
60 El Heraldo, July 8, 1950, p. 10.
61 Diario Gráfico February 13, 1951, p. 20.
62 El Tiempo, June 6, 1951, p. 11.
63 El Tiempo, May 3, 1951, p. 9.
64 Diario Gráfico, May 17, 1951, p. 19.
65 Diario Gráfico, June 2, 1951, p. 20.
66 El Tiempo, June 23, 1951, p. 16.
67 Diario Gráfico, July 11, 1951, p. 20.
68 Diario Gráfico, July 13, 1951, p. 19 and Diario Gráfico, December 1, 1951, p.19.
69 El Tiempo, September 28, 1950, p. 8.
70 Diario Gráfico, April 1, 1952, p. 18.
71 Diario Gráfico, April 19, 1952, p. 15.
72 Diario Gráfico, August 20, 1952, p. 20; Diario Gráfico, September 17, 1952, p. 22.
73 Diario Gráfico, February 17, 1951, p. 21.
74 Diario Gráfico, March 30, 1951, p. 22.
75 Diario Gráfico, December 8, 1952, p. 20.
76 Diario Gráfico, April 23, 1952, p. 20.

77 Diario Gráfico, April 21, 1952, p. 18.
78 Diario Gráfico, April 24, 1952, p. 15.
79 Diario Gráfico, April 16, 1952, p. 13.
80 Diario Gráfico, September 18, 1952, p. 18.
81 El Tiempo September 24, p. 10.
82 Diario Gráfico, October 16, 1952, p. 18.
83 El Tiempo, January 29, 1953, p. 10.
84 El Tiempo January 13, 1951, p. 11 & Diario Gráfico, December 22, 1951, p. 18.
85 El Tiempo, December 16, 1952, p. 9.
86 El Tiempo, December 19, 1952, p. 8.
87 El Heraldo, March 5, 1949, p. 8.
88 El Tiempo, February 28, 1951, p. 10.
89 El Tiempo, January 28, 1951, p. 14.
90 Diario Gráfico, March 2, 1951, p. 21.
91 Diario Gráfico, October 17, 1951, p. 18.
92 Diario Gráfico, November 14, 1951, p. 16.
93 Diario Gráfico, October 31, 1951, p. 18 and El Tiempo, October 31, 1951, p. 16.
94 Diario Gráfico, January 30, 1952, p. 16.
95 El Tiempo, February 1, 1952, p. 13.
96 Diario Gráfico, March 6, 1952, p. 19.
97 Diario Gráfico, April 2, 1952, p. 15.
98 Diario Gráfico, May 8, 1952, p. 13.
99 Diario Gráfico, May 8, 1952, p. 13.
100 Soutinho (2015), p. 189.
101 Diario Gráfico, April 22, 1952, p. 13.
102 El Tiempo, April 16, 193, p. 13.
103 El Tiempo, December 1, 1951, p. 10.
104 El Heraldo, September 17, 1949, p. 8.
105 El Heraldo, September 24, 1949, p. 8.
106 El Heraldo, February 14, 1950, p. 9.
107 El Tiempo, March 9, 1951, p. 10.
108 Diario Gráfico, April 21, 1952, p. 16.
109 Diario Gráfico, May 6, 1952, p. 13.
110 Diario Gráfico, March 29, 1951, p. 21.
111 El Tiempo, December 2, 1951, p. 10.
112 El Tiempo, December 17, 1952, p. 9.
113 El Tiempo, December 17, 1952, p. 9.
114 El Tiempo, December 17, 1952, p. 9.
115 Diario Gráfico March 13, 1952, p. 18.
116 Diario Gráfico, April 26, 1952, p. 14.
117 Diario Gráfico, December 13, 1951, p. 19.
118 El Tiempo, February 28, 1952, p. 10.
119 Diario Grafico, December 19, p. 18.
120 El Tiempo, February 16, 1953, p. 17.
121 Diario Gráfico, August 21, 1951, p. 19.
122 Diario Gráfico, June 25, 1951, p. 20.
123 El Tiempo, November 12, 1951, p. 11, and El Tiempo, November 22, 1951, p. 10.
124 El Tiempo, November 17, 1951, p. 10.
125 Diario Gráfico, March 11, 1952, p. 19.
126 Diario Gráfico, January 28, 1952, p. 20.
127 Diario Gráfico, December 22, 1950, p. 20.
128 El Tiempo, February 14, 1952, p. 10.
129 Diario Gráfico, March 10, 1952, p. 15.

130 Diario Gráfico, March 24, 1952, p. 18.
131 Diario Gráfico, October 3, 1952, p.17.
132 El Tiempo, November 25, 1952, p. 9.

## References

Adamson, R. (1996). *Bogota Bandit. The Outlaw Life of Charlie Mitten: Manchester United's Penalty King*. Mainstream Publishing Company.

Diario Gráfico. Various numbers. Biblioteca Luis Ángel Arango.

El Comercio. Various numbers. Biblioteca Nacional, and Instituto Riva Agüero, PUCP.

El Heraldo. Various numbers. Archive Diario El Heraldo.

El Mundo Deportivo. Various numbers. Available at https://www.mundodeportivo.com/hemeroteca

El Tiempo. Various Numbers. Available at https://news.google.com/newspapers?nid=N2osnxbUuuUC

La Crónica. Various Numbers. Biblioteca Nacional.

Potts Harmer, A. (2019). *England's Greatest Defender. The Untold Story of Neil Franklin*. Red Door.

Revista Goles. Various Numbers.

Soutinho, Felipe (2015). *San Pontoni del Papa. Vida y goles de un bendito del fútbol.* Felipe Soutinho.

# 4 The final curtain

## The shooting star: the Di Stéfano transfer

The Lima Pact formalized the unification of Colombian football under FIFA's jurisdiction. However, it was Article five, which prohibited transferring players to third parties without the "mutual agreement" of the original club, that would trigger the most complex financial operation of the era: the transfer of Alfredo Di Stéfano to Real Madrid. Both Real Madrid and Barcelona expressed interest in the Argentine genius immediately after the Millonarios' Madrid ballet exhibition. Although the Colombians rejected any potential deal, the Lima Pact implied that any arrangement required a tripartite agreement because River Plate remained the holder of the player's federative rights.

By late 1952, press rumors placed Di Stéfano and Néstor Rossi going back to River Plate, which was ultimately untrue. As the year vanished, Di Stéfano knew that both Barcelona and Real Madrid were interested in his services, and before signing a new contract with Millonarios, Di Stéfano had acknowledged that "Barcelona offered me, personally, 1,200,000 pesetas (USD 24,000 by the contemporary press accounts, USD 27,714 using the official exchange rate)".[1] At the time, Millonarios did not need money. Senior declared, "we will not sacrifice the team for any price".[2] Despite the interest of the Spaniards, Di Stéfano extended for one additional year his contract with Millonarios, whereby he would receive a USD 12,000 signing fee, not in December as the press had initially claimed, but on February 11, 1953.[3]

After that match in Curaçao, on February 22, 1953, Millonarios finally sent the players for vacation. Di Stéfano was tired of traveling; he had sent his wife back to Buenos Aires and decided not to show up for the start of the preseason tour in Chile in April. Having signed a contract, Alfonso Senior expected him to play the Chile and upcoming matches, especially because the club had paid USD 4,000 in advance. Di Stéfano acknowledges receiving the money. He claims in his biography that the money was to cover a four-month debt the club had with him from the 1952 season.[4] A couple of pages earlier, however, Di Stéfano acknowledged that they did "charge" for all the friendly

DOI: 10.4324/9781003396024-4

games, but that he was tired of them.[5] Moreover, Millonarios claimed that the club was a guarantor for COP 8,000 (USD 3,187) to the national government for the income tax, so that he could be allowed to leave the country.[6] Overall, given Millonarios' financial situation, it is difficult to believe that the club would pay him some overdue salaries and not pay anything in advance for the new contract. The point, in either case, is that then as now, when a player wants to leave, more often than not, he will.

Per the Lima Pact, Di Stéfano's rights belonged to Millonarios until October 15, 1954, but River Plate had to approve any transfer. On October 16, 1954, River Plate would be free to transfer the player without considering Millonarios' will. Barcelona decided to negotiate with River Plate.

Documentation preserved in River Plate's archive indicates that by May 1953, the two clubs were immersed in negotiations, treating the Lima Pact as an operative constraint rather than a merely symbolic sanction. River's initial demand valued the player at ARS 2,500,000 (USD 179,000). The agreement, settled at ARS 2,000,000 (USD 143,113), originally included a binding condition: Di Stéfano had to rejoin River Plate before July 26, 1953, and the Catalonians had to pay a first ARS 500,000 (USD 35,778) before August 11.

On May 23, Di Stéfano flew to Spain with FC Barcelona's sporting director, José Samitier. Di Stéfano, in his biography, backed by renowned Spanish sports journalists Enrique Ortego and Alfredo Relaño, writes that Barcelona paid "50%, 2,000,000 pesetas". Using an exchange rate of 43.3 pesetas per dollar for 1953, as reported by the *Banco de España*, implies a total valuation for the Argentine star of USD 92,379.[7] The figure is also close to the 4,400.000 pesetas (USD 101,617) that Zarama (2023) argues that Real Madrid paid in total to have Di Stéfano wearing white. The USD 143,113 figure from River Plate's archives is thus a novelty in the literature.

Santiago Bernabéu decided to bid for the star and, on July 25, sent River a telegram naming Raimundo Saporta as the man in charge of negotiating for Real Madrid. Barcelona, probably aware of Madrid's move, informed River Plate on July 30 that they were ready to honor the agreement. River would honor the deal with Barcelona, but if they did not come forward with the money before August 11, they would open negotiations with Real Madrid.

Meanwhile, Real Madrid was negotiating with Millonarios. Barcelona's agreement with River Plate guaranteed that Di Stéfano would play for them after October 1954, but to field him before, they had to settle with Millonarios. The Catalonians did not know it at the time, but they never had a chance of signing Di Stéfano. The bonds of friendship between Alfonso Senior and Santiago Bernabéu were too tight to think that Millonarios ever thought of selling the crack rights to Barcelona. Many years later, in 1977, Senior confessed that Bernabeu had told him that they needed Di Stéfano and that he had promised to sell it to him.[8]

On July 29, River Plate received a telegram from Bogota: "We respectfully inform you that we have reached full agreement with Real Madrid club to transfer him until October 1954". Six days earlier, the Colombian press was announcing the same thing. Taking advantage of Barcelona's presence in Venezuela, they opened negotiations with Millonarios. Press reports on July 23 announced that Real Madrid had agreed to pay COP 75,000 (29,880) plus the player's debt with Millonarios, around COP 14,000 (USD 5,577).[9] In September, Alfonso Senior admitted that Barcelona had offered COP 90,000 (USD 35,856), but he resented that the Catalonians had taken Di Stéfano to Spain while the player was under contract with the Colombians.[10] Years later, he declared that they had "offered or paid him USD 4,000" to convince him to move to Barcelona.[11]

River Plate's reply to Millonarios' telegram was immediate: "We hereby inform you that we are processing the definitive transfer of player Alfredo Di Stéfano with Club de Fútbol Barcelona". Records in River's archives show that the club received ARS 1,000,000 (USD 71,556) on August 7, 1953. That same day, River notified Millonarios, Barcelona, and AFA that the transfer was complete.

Real Madrid sent River Plate a telegram on August 11 as if Barcelona had not honored the agreement with the Argentines: "Without news from you. Deadline expired today. Communicate entry of our contract. Affectionate greeting". River replied immediately, informing that they had transferred Di Stéfano to Barcelona.

But Real Madrid knew that Barcelona had paid. On August 1, the club's director, Carlos Arjona, announced that Di Stéfano belonged to them because they had bought the rights to Millonarios until October 1954.[12] To reassure this, Alfonso Senior flew to Madrid, invited by Real Madrid on August 15, when, upon landing, he declared that Millonarios had not received any amount of money yet, but that the club was "morally obligated with Real Madrid".[13]

The negotiations must have been complex, as on August 17, Senior sent a telegram to Bogota stating that Di Stéfano belonged to Millonarios and that there were no negotiations with Real Madrid. However, when he returned to Bogota on August 25, there was now a contract between Millonarios and Real Madrid.

Di Stéfano's own account of the situation reflects the uncertainty of the period.[14] He was in Barcelona, but could not play because Real Madrid had the rights for him to play before October 1954. Things got even more complicated when, on August 24, the Spanish Sports National Delegation announced that foreign players were not authorized to play in Spain. In early September, Enrique Pardo, River Plate's president, announced that the club would not return the ARS 2,000,000 (USD 143,113) that Barcelona had paid, because, once sold, any contingencies were the Spanish club's problem.[15]

Di Stéfano could not play because he was a foreigner and because two clubs claimed rights to his talent. FIFA, via Armando Muñoz Calero, former President of the Spanish Football Federation, announced on September 15 that Di Stéfano would play for Real Madrid during the 1953/1954 season.

The following season, 1954/1955, he would move to Barcelona, then back to Madrid for the 1955/1956 season, and finally to Barcelona for the 1956/1957 season, a Solomonic but ridiculous decision. Barcelona eventually rejected the decision. The final obstacle was removed on September 18, when the National Sports Delegation decided that foreign players whose negotiations began before August 22 could play in Spain.[16]

Di Stéfano signed a four-year contract and made his debut with Real Madrid on September 23, 1953, in a friendly match against Nancy. He arrived overweight from Barcelona, scored a header, and would forever change the history of Real Madrid.

Real Madrid reimbursed Barcelona—including an undisclosed bonus—for what it had paid River Plate and compensated Millonarios, covering Di Stéfano's debt as well. The total came to around USD 178,000—approximately USD 2,146,286 in 2025 dollars. The price of a star. This significant financial operation revealed not merely a chaotic flight of talent, but rather a structured sequence defined by contractual deadlines, transfer fees, and the cross-border coordination mechanisms—however imperfect—established by the Lima Pact.

## Lessons from El Dorado

The history of El Dorado has traditionally been told through the lens of sporting epic and biographical anecdotes, focusing on the arrival of world-class stars to a peripheral league. However, a rigorous examination of the financial balances and hiring flows between 1949 and 1953 reveals a different narrative. What occurred was not a spontaneous miracle but a classic cycle of a speculative bubble: an initial disruptive innovation followed by an unsustainable process of imitation in a market with artificially low barriers to entry and demand that, in practice, did not expand proportionally with the escalating quality and cost of the product. From the perspective of industrial organization, the rise and fall of this period can be understood as a phenomenon of creative destruction, in which the financial collapse of individual firms was the necessary price for the creation of a new industry.

The origins of this economic cycle lie in massive market failures in South American football: the players' strike in Argentina and Uruguay, and the lack of professional regulation in Peru and Paraguay. Add to this recipe the inequities of the English labor market, the restrictions on freedom under Hungary's and other communist regimes, and the visionary audacity of club directors with little regard to protocol, and we have all the key elements for a unique experiment at the margins of world football.

In this context, Millonarios, under Alfonso Senior, acted as the "first mover", identifying an arbitrage opportunity that altered the industry's cost structure. By operating outside FIFA's jurisdiction, Colombian clubs eliminated the industry's most significant capital cost: transfer fees. Although many stars arrived as free agents in a modern sense, the realities of the labor market at the time meant they were defying the tradition and norms of the football world. They arrived without the hiring club paying a single peso to their club of origin for their federative rights. Mega stars like Alfredo Di Stéfano or Néstor Raúl Rossi arrived at Millonarios without River Plate receiving a peso, as happened to San Lorenzo when Rial or Pontoni signed for Santa Fe.

Furthermore, the infrastructure's fixed costs were heavily subsidized. Stadiums such as El Campín in Bogotá and Pascual Guerrero in Cali were public goods funded by some linear combination of local and national funds rather than by the clubs themselves. This structure transformed football into an industry intensive in human capital but with low sunk costs, allowing for a product of exceptionally high quality with an operating margin that, in principle, could only be sustainable with a robust demand.

The financial and sporting success of the Millonarios model, established in 1949, sent a powerful signal to the rest of the market, triggering what behavioral economics calls herding behavior. First, larger markets, such as Cali, then clubs in smaller markets, such as Cúcuta Deportivo, Deportivo Pereira, and Junior, attempted to replicate Millonarios' business model without possessing the necessary economies of scale. Cali brought the best Peruvians, Cúcuta imported Uruguayans, including world champions, Pereira hired Paraguayan national team players, and Junior brought Brazilian megastar Heleno de Freitas. This collective imitation fell into the fallacy of composition: what was rational for a dominant firm in the wealthiest city became irrational when adopted simultaneously in smaller markets. The resulting bidding war for talent inflated salaries to global levels, while the demand—ticket sales—in cities like Manizales, Barranquilla, and even Medellín, lacked the depth to sustain such high variable costs. Santa Fe's and Universidad's eventual failure further proved that even in the largest local market, it was difficult to replicate the model. Evidence of the imbalance is the high mortality rate of clubs: Sporting, Huracán, Medellín, and Universidad faced liquidity crises and even disappeared.

This fragility was exacerbated by the strategic complementarity inherent in the sports industry. A team cannot produce its product in isolation; the value of a match depends heavily on the quality of the opponent. To maintain the public interest that justified high payrolls, Millonarios needed rivals of comparable stature. The league's revenue-sharing system functioned as an inefficient cross-subsidy from large to small teams. Even powerful clubs like Boca Juniors became financially dependent on Millonarios' visits to balance their books.

The cycle reached its turning point with a regulatory shock: the 1951 Lima Pact. From Colombia's standpoint, it was the result of the insufficient demand to cover the escalating costs. As market leaders saw the opportunity to export services through international tours, the strategy cannibalized the domestic product, exhausting workers in an ever-increasing number of games and trips, while the domestic tournament lost value, depressing the revenue of the smaller clubs that depended on it.

The Lima Pact reestablished property rights over players, transforming the industry's horizon. By setting a deadline for the return of foreign players to their homeland in October 1954, the pact effectively placed an expiration date on the clubs' main assets, disincentivizing long-term investment. It introduced an entry barrier, effectively ending the era of free talent acquisition. The bubble burst because all factors corrected the exuberant expectations. The contraction of the league, which went from 18 teams in 1951 to just 10 in 1954, reflects a harsh market correction with inefficient firms purged.

Despite the financial turmoil, El Dorado can be characterized as a productive bubble. Much as the railway mania of the nineteenth century in the USA, the collapse of individual firms did not lead to the industry's disappearance. On the contrary, the legacy of this period was the construction of a robust institutional infrastructure. In a span of five years, Colombia transitioned from a disjointed amateurism to a consolidated professional league, developing a national market integrated by air transport and establishing a globally recognized brand. The entrepreneurs of El Dorado took risks, and many failed, but in their attempt, they founded a modern entertainment industry that persisted long after the foreign stars had departed.

The Colombian league during El Dorado was arguably the first multinational league in football history. We have presented and discussed the pull and push factors that allowed a league to host some of the most talented players of their generation. Whatever the reasons, yesterday as today, what made the difference was the promise of riches never seen before in the football stage. Money, turns out, had the power to globalize an industry in a world yet to embrace globalization. Others have followed suit.

In the early 1990s, Japan lured Zico, one of the world's top stars of the 1980s. Well into his thirties, Zico opened a new frontier in football. Years later, India, China, and Qatar invested heavily to bring other aging stars. Roberto Carlos and Alessandro Del Piero in India, Carlos Tévez and Didier Drogba in China, Xavi Hernández and James Rodríguez in Qatar, all arrived for different reasons, money one of them. David Beckham, in 2007, became the flagship for the MLS, as did Cristiano Ronaldo for the Saudi Pro League in 2022. While some of these leagues have disappeared from the front seat of the world stage, others keep pushing hard to become representative leagues. They all have in common that, as Millonarios did with Pedernera, the first major footballer to join the project was an aging star.

El Dorado taught that the stars make an excellent first impression and are necessary to attract other, sometimes younger, top players. However, the biggest lesson is that it is very difficult, if not impossible, to build a sustainable project without a long-term structure, both sporting and financial. History tends to repeat itself. Consider the Saudi league. In February 2026, Ronaldo went on strike for two games. There were clear football reasons, as he was asking for reinforcements. But rumors also suggest that his club had overdue wages owed to some employees. If Cristiano leaves, the media attention on the league would collapse.

During El Dorado, rumors of Colombian teams wanting to bring in Ladislao Kubala, Antoni Ramallets, Obdulio Varela, or other top stars were constant. In some cases, the clubs were in fact attempting to do it. However, while money is a significant factor, sporting considerations mattered then and matter now. Di Stéfano had a future in Spain. He realized that the golden ribbons of El Dorado were over. It is preferable to construct a project on solid foundations rather than commence with the superstructure, expecting to fortify the base subsequently.

The history of El Dorado does not teach how to develop a successful league in the football-developing world. It does give a lesson on how not to do it. And one could argue that the simple lesson is still not well understood.

## Notes

1 Diario Gráfico, December 3, 1952, p. 12.
2 Diario Gráfico, December 3, 1952, p. 12.
3 El Tiempo, April 12, 1953, p. 11.
4 Di Stéfano (2000), p. 112.
5 Di Stéfano (2000), p. 110.
6 El Tiempo, April 11, 1953, p. 10.
7 https://repositorio.bde.es/handle/123456789/15657 visited February 7, 2026.
8 El Tiempo, June 20, 1977, p. última C.
9 El Tiempo, July 23, 1953, p. 13.
10 El Tiempo, September 12, 1953, p. 16.
11 El Tiempo, June 20, 1977, p. última C.
12 El Tiempo, August 2, 1953, p. 10.
13 El Tiempo, August 16, 1953, p. 11.
14 Lorente (1954).
15 Diario Gráfico, September 4, 1953, p. 16.
16 Tovar (2014).

## References

Di Stéfano. A. (2000). *Gracias Vieja*. Aguilar Editores.
Diario Gráfico. Various numbers. Biblioteca Luis Ángel Arango.
El Tiempo. Various Numbers. Available at https://news.google.com/newspapers?nid=N2osnxbUuuUC.
Lorente, R. (1954). *Di Stéfano cuenta su vida*. Lifesa.
Tovar, J. (2014). *Números redondos*. Grijalbo.

# 5 Data and archival research

The information on our main attendance and gate receipts is compiled from multiple sources. Diario El Comercio (Instituto Riva Agüero and Biblioteca Nacional, Lima), Diario Gráfico (Biblioteca Luis Ángel Arango, Bogota), El Heraldo (archives in Barranquilla), El Tiempo (online https://news.google.com/newspapers), La Crónica (Biblioteca Nacional, Lima), Revista Goles, Revista Cromos (Biblioteca Nacional, Bogota), Revista El Gráfico (Biblioteca Nacional, Buenos Aires), Revista River Plate (River Plate Archive, Buenos Aires), and Revista Semana (Biblioteca Nacional, Bogota).

In addition to the above, we gathered salaries and other information from the ABC newspaper (https://www.abc.es/archivo/periodicos/), Archivo General de la Nación (Bogota), El Mundo Deportivo (online https://www.mundodeportivo.com/hemeroteca), and https://news.google.com/newspapers.

The exchange rates used are presented in Table 5.1.

DOI: 10.4324/9781003396024-5

*Table 5.1* Exchange rate local currency / 1USD

| *Month* | *Argentina* | *Colombia* | *Peru* | *Mexico* | *Uruguay*[a] | *Ecuador* | *UK* |
|---|---|---|---|---|---|---|---|
| January-48 | 4.030 | 1.750 | 13.172 | | 2.11 | 17.91 | 0.2481389580 |
| February-48 | 4.026 | 1.750 | 14.447 | | 2.11 | 17.46 | 0.2481389580 |
| March-48 | 4.014 | 1.750 | 15.867 | | 2.11 | 16.86 | 0.2481389580 |
| April-48 | 4.011 | 1.750 | 16.673 | | 2.11 | 16.96 | 0.2481389580 |
| May-48 | 4.017 | 1.750 | 16.842 | | 2.11 | 16.89 | 0.2481389580 |
| June-48 | 4.017 | 1.750 | 17.973 | | 2.11 | 17.8 | 0.2481389580 |
| July-48 | 4.861 | 1.750 | 17.332 | | 2.11 | 18.23 | 0.2481389580 |
| August-48 | 4.810 | 1.750 | 16.772 | | 2.11 | 18.73 | 0.2481389580 |
| September-48 | 4.835 | 1.750 | 16.044 | | 2.11 | 18.25 | 0.2481389580 |
| October-48 | 4.885 | 1.750 | 15.942 | | 2.11 | 18.25 | 0.2481389580 |
| November-48 | 4.857 | 1.750 | 14.987 | | 2.11 | 17.96 | 0.2481389580 |
| December-48 | 4.814 | 1.820 | 15.208 | | 2.11 | 17.75 | 0.2481389580 |
| January-49 | 4.852 | 1.960 | 14.996 | | 2.69 | 17.55 | 0.2481389580 |
| February-49 | 4.810 | 1.960 | 15.047 | | 2.69 | 17.11 | 0.2481389580 |
| March-49 | 4.810 | 1.960 | 15.136 | | 2.69 | 17.15 | 0.2481389580 |
| April-49 | 4.810 | 1.960 | 14.989 | | 2.69 | 17.01 | 0.2481389580 |
| May-49 | 4.810 | 1.960 | 14.827 | | 2.69 | 16.85 | 0.2481389580 |
| June-49 | 4.810 | 1.960 | 14.736 | | 2.69 | 16.75 | 0.2481389580 |
| July-49 | 4.810 | 1.960 | 14.619 | | 2.69 | 17.26 | 0.2481389580 |
| August-49 | 4.810 | 1.960 | 14.983 | | 2.69 | 17.25 | 0.2481389580 |
| September-49 | 4.810 | 1.960 | 15.027 | | 2.69 | 17.52 | 0.2906976740 |
| October-49 | 9.020 | 1.960 | 15.536 | | 2.69 | 18.09 | 0.3571428570 |
| November-49 | 9.020 | 1.960 | 15.402 | | 2.69 | 18.21 | 0.3571428570 |
| December-49 | 9.020 | 1.960 | 15.370 | | 2.69 | 18.14 | 0.3571428570 |
| January-50 | 9.020 | 1.960 | 15.560 | 8.641 | 2.6 | 18.11 | 0.3571428570 |
| February-50 | 9.020 | 1.960 | 15.730 | 8.641 | 2.6 | 17.53 | 0.3571428570 |

(Continued)

*Table 5.1* (Continued)

| *Month* | *Argentina* | *Colombia* | *Peru* | *Mexico* | *Uruguay*[a] | *Ecuador* | *UK* |
|---|---|---|---|---|---|---|---|
| March-50 | 9.020 | 1.960 | 15.710 | 8.642 | 2.6 | 17.01 | 0.3571428570 |
| April-50 | 9.020 | 1.960 | 15.660 | 8.647 | 2.6 | 16.78 | 0.3571428570 |
| May-50 | 9.020 | 1.960 | 15.090 | 8.648 | 2.6 | 17.28 | 0.3571428570 |
| June-50 | 9.020 | 1.960 | 15.000 | 8.649 | 2.6 | 17.77 | 0.3571428570 |
| July-50 | 9.020 | 1.960 | 14.890 | 8.642 | 2.6 | 18.17 | 0.3571428570 |
| August-50 | 9.771 | 1.960 | 15.150 | 8.64 | 2.6 | 19.05 | 0.3571428570 |
| September-50 | 13.679 | 1.960 | 15.760 | 8.642 | 2.6 | 19.27 | 0.3571428570 |
| October-50 | 13.634 | 1.960 | 15.040 | 8.641 | 2.6 | 19.63 | 0.3571428570 |
| November-50 | 14.078 | 1.960 | 14.890 | 8.64 | 2.6 | 19.24 | 0.3571428570 |
| December-50 | 14.384 | 1.960 | 14.970 | 8.643 | 2.6 | 18.31 | 0.3571428570 |
| January-51 | 14.048 | 1.960 | 14.840 | 8.644 | 2.26 | 17.92 | 0.3571428570 |
| February-51 | 14.030 | 1.960 | 14.730 | 8.646 | 2.26 | 18.1 | 0.3571428570 |
| March-51 | 14.077 | 2.150 | 14.640 | 8.642 | 2.26 | 17.61 | 0.3571428570 |
| April-51 | 14.046 | 2.510 | 14.880 | 8.65 | 2.26 | 17.67 | 0.3571428570 |
| May-51 | 14.173 | 2.510 | 15.230 | 8.65 | 2.26 | 17.59 | 0.3571428570 |
| June-51 | 14.141 | 2.510 | 15.060 | 8.65 | 2.26 | 17.59 | 0.3571428570 |
| July-51 | 14.058 | 2.510 | 15.370 | 8.65 | 2.26 | 17.48 | 0.3571428570 |
| August-51 | 14.152 | 2.510 | 15.220 | 8.644 | 2.26 | 17.62 | 0.3571428570 |
| September-51 | 14.418 | 2.510 | 15.180 | 8.642 | 2.26 | 17.83 | 0.3571428570 |
| October-51 | 14.407 | 2.510 | 15.260 | 8.65 | 2.26 | 17.8 | 0.3571428570 |
| November-51 | 14.455 | 2.510 | 15.150 | 8.646 | 2.26 | 17.52 | 0.3571428570 |
| December-51 | 14.344 | 2.510 | 15.070 | 8.648 | 2.26 | 17.25 | 0.3571428570 |
| January-52 | 14.344 | 2.510 | 15.130 | 8.648 | 2.67 | 17.28 | 0.3597122300 |
| February-52 | 14.138 | 2.510 | 15.150 | 8.649 | 2.67 | 17.28 | 0.3597122300 |
| March-52 | 14.030 | 2.510 | 15.070 | 8.645 | 2.67 | 17.31 | 0.3571428570 |
| April-52 | 14.030 | 2.510 | 14.930 | 8.645 | 2.67 | 17.29 | 0.3558718860 |
| May-52 | 14.010 | 2.510 | 14.960 | 8.647 | 2.67 | 17.29 | 0.3571428570 |
| June-52 | 13.977 | 2.510 | 15.070 | 8.65 | 2.67 | 17.3 | 0.3584229390 |

| | | | | | | | |
|---|---|---|---|---|---|---|---|
| July-52 | 13.976 | 2.510 | 15.120 | 8.638 | 2.67 | 17.48 | 0.3584229390 |
| August-52 | 13.975 | 2.510 | 14.980 | 8.603 | 2.67 | 17.36 | 0.3584229390 |
| September-52 | 13.975 | 2.510 | 15.260 | 8.604 | 2.67 | 17.37 | 0.3597122300 |
| October-52 | 13.975 | 2.510 | 15.530 | 8.613 | 2.67 | 17.39 | 0.3584229390 |
| November-52 | 13.975 | 2.510 | 15.480 | 8.601 | 2.67 | 17.4 | 0.3571428570 |
| December-52 | 13.975 | 2.510 | 15.370 | 8.601 | 2.67 | 17.36 | 0.3558718860 |
| January-53 | 13.975 | 2.510 | 15.680 | 8.601 | 2.92 | 17.32 | 0.3558718860 |
| February-53 | 13.975 | 2.510 | 16.840 | 8.607 | 2.92 | 17.29 | 0.3546099290 |
| March-53 | 13.975 | 2.510 | 18.070 | 8.609 | 2.92 | 17.28 | 0.3546099290 |
| April-53 | 13.975 | 2.510 | 20.560 | 8.614 | 2.92 | 17.28 | 0.3546099290 |
| May-53 | 13.975 | 2.510 | 20.050 | 8.648 | 2.92 | 17.34 | 0.3558718860 |
| June-53 | 13.975 | 2.510 | 19.570 | 8.65 | 2.92 | 17.37 | 0.3558718860 |
| July-53 | 13.975 | 2.510 | 19.230 | 8.626 | 2.92 | 17.38 | 0.3546099290 |
| August-53 | 13.975 | 2.510 | 19.230 | 8.607 | 2.92 | 17.32 | 0.3546099290 |
| September-53 | 13.975 | 2.510 | 19.230 | 8.609 | 2.92 | 17.35 | 0.3571428570 |
| October-53 | 13.975 | 2.510 | 19.230 | 8.603 | 2.92 | 17.39 | 0.3558718860 |
| November-53 | 13.975 | 2.510 | 19.230 | 8.601 | 2.92 | 17.37 | 0.3558718860 |
| December-53 | 13.975 | 2.510 | 19.230 | 8.601 | 2.92 | 17.35 | 0.3558718860 |
| January-54 | 13.975 | 2.510 | 19.230 | 8.606 | 3.19 | 17.37 | 0.3558718860 |
| February-54 | 13.976 | 2.510 | 19.230 | 8.609 | 3.19 | 17.36 | 0.3558718860 |
| March-54 | 13.975 | 2.510 | 19.230 | 8.614 | 3.19 | 17.31 | 0.3546099290 |
| April-54 | 13.975 | 2.510 | 19.230 | 10.173 | 3.19 | 17.3 | 0.3546099290 |
| May-54 | 13.975 | 2.510 | 19.230 | 12.51 | 3.19 | 17.32 | 0.3546099290 |
| June-54 | 13.975 | 2.510 | 19.230 | 12.51 | 3.19 | 17.32 | 0.3546099290 |
| July-54 | 13.975 | 2.510 | 19.230 | 12.501 | 3.19 | 17.31 | 0.3546099290 |
| August-54 | 13.975 | 2.510 | 19.230 | 12.491 | 3.19 | 17.31 | 0.3558718860 |
| September-54 | 13.975 | 2.510 | 19.230 | 12.491 | 3.19 | 17.31 | 0.3571428570 |
| October-54 | 13.975 | 2.510 | 19.230 | 12.491 | 3.19 | 17.35 | 0.3571428570 |
| November-54 | 13.976 | 2.510 | 19.230 | 12.491 | 3.19 | 17.35 | 0.3584229390 |
| December-54 | 13.975 | 2.510 | 19.230 | 12.491 | 3.19 | 17.33 | 0.3584229390 |
| January-55 | 13.975 | 2.510 | 19.230 | 12.491 | 3.38 | 17.31 | 0.3584229390 |
| February-55 | 13.975 | 2.510 | 19.230 | 12.491 | 3.38 | 17.3 | 0.3597122300 |

(Continued)

*Table 5.1* (Continued)

| *Month* | *Argentina* | *Colombia* | *Peru* | *Mexico* | *Uruguay*[a] | *Ecuador* | *UK* |
|---|---|---|---|---|---|---|---|
| March-55 | 13.975 | 2.510 | 19.230 | 12.491 | 3.38 | 17.31 | 0.3584229390 |
| April-55 | 13.975 | 2.510 | 19.230 | 12.491 | 3.38 | 17.31 | 0.3571428570 |
| May-55 | 13.991 | 2.510 | 19.230 | 12.491 | 3.38 | 17.34 | 0.3571428570 |
| June-55 | 13.976 | 2.510 | 19.230 | 12.491 | 3.38 | 17.35 | 0.3584229390 |
| July-55 | 13.977 | 2.510 | 19.230 | 12.491 | 3.38 | 17.61 | 0.3584229390 |
| August-55 | 13.981 | 2.510 | 19.230 | 12.491 | 3.38 | 17.63 | 0.3584229390 |
| September-55 | 13.976 | 2.510 | 19.230 | 12.491 | 3.38 | 17.39 | 0.3584229390 |
| October-55 | 13.982 | 2.510 | 19.230 | 12.491 | 3.38 | 17.31 | 0.3584229390 |
| November-55 | 32.610 | 2.510 | 19.230 | 12.491 | 3.38 | 17.31 | 0.3571428570 |
| December-55 | 35.890 | 2.510 | 19.230 | 12.491 | 3.38 | 17.34 | 0.3571428570 |
| January-56 | 39.530 | 2.510 | 19.230 | 12.491 | 4.05 | 17.37 | 0.3558718860 |
| February-56 | 42.610 | 2.510 | 19.230 | 12.491 | 4.05 | 17.53 | 0.3558718860 |
| March-56 | 40.770 | 2.510 | 19.230 | 12.491 | 4.05 | 17.65 | 0.3558718860 |
| April-56 | 39.490 | 2.510 | 19.230 | 12.491 | 4.05 | 17.86 | 0.3558718860 |
| May-56 | 37.240 | 2.510 | 19.230 | 12.491 | 4.05 | 18.28 | 0.3558718860 |
| June-56 | 33.810 | 2.510 | 19.230 | 12.491 | 4.05 | 18.57 | 0.3571428570 |
| July-56 | 31.930 | 2.510 | 19.230 | 12.491 | 4.05 | 18.57 | 0.3584229390 |
| August-56 | 30.650 | 2.510 | 19.230 | 12.491 | 4.05 | 18.8 | 0.3597122300 |
| September-56 | 31.490 | 2.510 | 19.230 | 12.491 | 4.05 | 19.13 | 0.3597122300 |
| October-56 | 31.730 | 2.510 | 19.230 | 12.491 | 4.05 | 19.37 | 0.3584229390 |
| November-56 | 34.180 | 2.510 | 19.230 | 12.491 | 4.05 | 18.88 | 0.3597122300 |
| December-56 | 35.860 | 2.510 | 19.230 | 12.491 | 4.05 | 18.71 | 0.3584229390 |

[a] For Uruguay, we take the average annual free-market exchange rate, monthly data were not available.

*Sources:* Colombia: Banco de la República de Colomba, Series históricas sector externo.

Argentina: Banco Central de la República de Argentina, Series históricas Apéndice 8.

Mexico: Banco de México, Informes anuales.

Uruguay: Facueltad de ciencias sociales Universdiad de la República, Tipo de cambio real 1913–2003.

Ecuador: Banco Central del Ecuador, "Sucres por U.S Dólar" (2001).

# Index

Note: **Bold** page numbers refer to tables and *italic* page numbers refer to figures.

For Product Safety Concerns and Information please contact our EU representative GPSR@taylorandfrancis.com
Taylor & Francis Verlag GmbH, Kaufingerstraße 24, 80331 München, Germany

www.ingramcontent.com/pod-product-compliance
Lightning Source LLC
LaVergne TN
LVHW011512200926
848484LV00001B/27
*9781032499062*